S0-AAZ-861

THE UNITED STATES: A Christian Nation

The MISSION of American Vision, Inc. is to publish and distribute books that lead individuals toward:

* A personal faith in the one true God: Father, Son, and Holy Spirit

* A lifestyle of practical discipleship

* A worldview that is consistent with the historic Christian faith

* An ability to apply the Bible to all of life.

© 1905 by the John D. Winston company, Philadelphia, Pennsylvania
© 1996 by American Vision, Inc. All rights reserved.
Published October 1996.
Printed in the United States of America.

Note: Misspellings and typographical errors have been corrected. In addition, subheadings have been added and occasional minor editorial revisions have been made to Brewer's text to clarify the material for the modern reader.

American Vision, Inc.
2512 Cobb Parkway
Smyrna, Georgia 30080

Cover design and typesetting:
James Talmage / JET Studio
Byron, Georgia

Cover portrait: David Josiah Brewer by Robert Lea MacCameron. Courtesy of the Supreme Court of the United States

LIBRARY OF CONGRESS CATALOGING-IN-PUBLICATION DATA
Brewer, David J.
    The United States: A Christian Nation / David Josiah Brewer
    Includes an introduction by Gary DeMar; biographical information by J. Robert Brame, III; the U.S. Supreme Court case Church of the Holy Trinity vs. United States; and a commentary on the Holy Trinity case by Dr. Herbert W. Titus.
    ISBN: 0-915815-20-6
    1. History 2. Religion (Christianity) 3. Church / State

THE UNITED STATES: A Christian Nation

DAVID J. BREWER

Associate Justice of the Supreme Court

The John C. Winston Company
1905

This edition published by
American Vision
1996

Contents

Introduction

By Gary DeMar

ROBERT BOSTON, ASSISTANT DIRECTOR OF COMMUNICATIONS FOR Americans United for Separation of Church and State, writes that David Brewer's *The United States a Christian Nation* "is very interesting, and needless to say, never quoted by the Religious Right since it is completely at odds with their view."[1] Brewer was the Supreme Court Justice who proclaimed in *The Church of the Holy Trinity vs. United States* (1892) that America is a "Christian nation."

Boston's conclusions have no basis in fact. I was not aware that Brewer's book even existed until I saw it referenced in Stephen L. Carter's *The Culture of Disbelief,* and that only in a note.[2] Robert T. Handy also referred to Brewer's book in *Undermined Establishment: Church-State Relations in America, 1880–1920,* also only in a note.[3] Once I knew of Brewer's book, I located a copy, read it, quoted extensively from it in *America's Christian History,* and found that it supported what advocates of America's Christian history have been saying for years.

Boston leaves the impression that secular advocates of church-state separation are well aware of Brewer's book and interact with it. Such is not the case. For example, in the "Suggestions for Further Reading Section" in his own book, Boston lists Leo Pfeffer's *Church, State and Freedom* (1967) as a "classic volume" that "thoroughly examines the history behind the religion clause of the Constitution and looks at contemporary church-state issues."[4] This "classic volume" nowhere refers to Brewer's book, neither in the five-page "Selected Bibliography" (650–54) nor in its discussion of Brewer's *Church of the Holy Trinity vs. United States* ruling.

Anson Phelps Stokes and Leo Pfeffer co-authored *Church and State in the United States,* a revised and updated one-volume edition of the original three-volume work.[5] Like *Church, State and Freedom,* the nine-page bibliography of this book does not mention Brewer. In its discussion of *Church of the Holy Trinity vs. United States* and the Christian nation thesis, Stokes and Pfeffer neglect to cite Brewer's book. How can Boston accuse "Religious Right" authors of never quoting Brewer's book when authors and books he recommends do not mention it, list it in their bibliographies, or interact with it?

Boston claims that Brewer's book "is completely at odds" with the views of the Christian Right, that is, with those who maintain that America was founded as a Christian nation. Boston writes, quoting Brewer:

> "But in what sense can [the United States] be called a Christian nation?" asked Brewer. "Not in the sense that Christianity is the established religion or the people are compelled in any manner to support it. On the contrary, the Constitution specifically provides that 'Congress shall make no law respecting an establishment of religion or prohibiting the free exercise thereof.' Neither is it Christian in the sense that all its citizens are either in fact or in name Christians. On the contrary, all religions have free scope within its borders. Numbers of our people profess other religions, and many reject all."[6]

As far as I know, advocates of the Christian America thesis do not believe that the State should compel people to become Christians or have tax monies collected to support churches. Moreover, the Christian America thesis is not dependent upon the idea "that all its citizens are either in fact or in name Christians." Brewer is simply supporting the constitutional doctrine that Congress — America's only national legislative body — is prohibited from establishing a single Christian denomination as the nation's tax-supported religion. If Brewer does not mean this, then why does he, for example, commend Maryland's 1776 constitution which states that "the legislature may, in their discretion, lay a general and equal tax, for the support of the Christian religion"?[7] Furthermore, why does Brewer recount that "in several colonies and states a profession of the Christian faith was made an indispensable condition to holding office."[8] He even mentions North Carolina's constitution that remained in force until 1868, eighty years after the drafting of the United States Constitution and the First Amendment. North Carolina's Constitution reads in part: "That no person who shall deny the being of God or the truth of the Christian religion, or the divine authority either of the Old or New Testaments, or who shall hold religious principles incompatible with the freedom and safety of the State, shall be capable of holding any office or place of trust or profit in the civil department within this State."[9] States were permitted to require a religious test for office holders, a stipulation that Brewer does not refute or take issue with.

Brewer states that the people are not compelled "in any manner to support" the Christian religion, and yet he asserts that the setting aside of Sunday "from the other days as a day of rest is enforced by the legislation of nearly all if not all the States of the Union."[10] Notice that the legislation is enforced. Enforcement is the prerogative of civil government and its courts. Brewer summarizes the historical record this way: "By these and other evidences I claim to have shown that the calling of this republic a Christian nation is not a mere pretence but a recognition of an historical, legal and social truth."[11]

Boston first uses Brewer against "Religious Right" supporters by claiming that his position is "completely at odds with their view."[12] Then he turns around and maintains that the *Holy Trinity* case is "a legal anomaly," an "obscure ruling that has no bearing on the type of church-state relationship the Framers intended for this nation." He goes on to claim that it "cannot seriously be considered today as [an] appropriate guideline for American society."[13] So which is it? Does Brewer support or oppose the agenda of Americans United and other secular advocates? Let the reader decide by carefully reading this new edition of David Brewer's *The United States a Christian Nation.*

While Brewer makes it clear that America was founded as a Christian nation, there are places where we disagree with some of his assessments and conclusions. We felt, however, that the overwhelming impact of his arguments on the Christian America thesis was enough to warrant a reprint, despite the few instances where there are differences of opinion.

NOTES

1. Robert Boston, *Why the Religious Right is Wrong About Separation of Church and State* (Buffalo, NY: Prometheus Books, 1993), 84.

2. Stephen L. Carter, *The Culture of Disbelief: How American Law and Politics Trivialize Religious Devotion* (New York: Anchor/Doubleday, [1993] 1994), 292, note 8.

3. Robert T. Handy, *Undermined Establishment: Church-State Relations in America, 1880–1920* (Lawrenceville, NJ: Princeton University Press, 1991), 13, note 11.

4. Boston, *Why the Religious Right is Wrong*, 245.

5. Anson Phelps Stokes and Leo Pfeffer, *Church and State in the United States*, revised one-volume edition (New York: Harper and Row, [1950] 1964).

6. Boston, *Why the Religious Right is Wrong*, 245. Brewer's quotation is found on page 12 of the original edition of *The United States: A Christian Nation* (Philadelphia, PA: The John C. Winston Co., 1905) and page ** of this edition.

7. Brewer, *United States: A Christian Nation*, 22.

8. Brewer, *United States: A Christian Nation*, 22.

9. Brewer, *United States: A Christian Nation*, 24.

10. Brewer, *United States: A Christian Nation*, 56.

11. Brewer, *United States: A Christian Nation*, 46.

12. Boston, *Why the Religious Right is Wrong*, 85.

13. Boston, *Why the Religious Right is Wrong*, 85.

David Josiah Brewer

(1837–1910)

BY J. ROBERT BRAME, III

U.S. Supreme Court Justice David Josiah Brewer

David Josiah Brewer

(1837–1910)

By J. Robert Brame, III

BACKGROUND

David Josiah Brewer was born June 20, 1837, in Smyrna, Asia Minor, of missionary parents. His parents returned to America during his early years, and at the age of fifteen he entered Wesleyan College in Connecticut. After two years, he transferred to his family's school, Yale College. He graduated at nineteen, read law, and then attended the Albany Law School.

After being admitted to the Bar of New York, Brewer headed west, first as a miner seeking gold around Pike's Peak and then as a resident of Levenworth, Kansas. In Kansas, he settled down and held a succession of public jobs. In 1862, he was persuaded to stand for election as Judge of the Probate and Criminal Court. He was elected and thereafter served for almost 46 years in various judicial capacities, including the First Judicial District of Kansas, the Kansas Supreme Court (1870–1884), the 8th Circuit Federal Court of Appeals (1884–1889) and the U.S. Supreme Court (1889–1910).

CHARACTER

Brewer had a ready wit and warm personal manner. Following his death, the Chief Justice of the U.S. Supreme Court commented on the "ineffable sweetness of [Brewer's] disposition..." and noted that in Brewer "the foundation of tears and the foundation of laughter ran close together."[1] A resolution drafted by the Bar of the United States Supreme Court and delivered by the Attorney General of the United States noted Brewer's integrity: "No one ever doubted his purity of life, his integrity of purpose, and his profound intellect."

In a eulogy recorded in the official reports of the U.S. Supreme Court, the Attorney General of the United States commented that Brewer was the son of a Christian missionary "and the son's life, like the father's, was one of service." He concluded the eulogy by quoting Deuteronomy 1:17: "Ye shall not respect persons in judgment; but ye shall hear the small as well as the great; ye shall not be afraid of the face of man, for the judgment is God's."

The story of Brewer's appointment to the Supreme Court reveals a mature Christian character. President Harrison had narrowed his choice to Brewer and one of Brewer's Yale classmates, Henry Brown. While Brewer's friends were campaigning for him, Brewer wrote a letter in support of Brown. When President Harrison heard of the letter, he was reportedly so impressed by Brewer's generosity that he chose Brewer for the nomination.[2]

FAITH AND WORK

Following his appointment to the U.S. Supreme Court, Brewer became a prolific writer and speaker on a wide range of public issues. In addition to authoring more than 700 judicial opinions, Brewer wrote four books and monographs and delivered speeches and lectures almost without number. In addition to judicial duties and writing, he remained involved in other activities. For example, he presided over a Congressional Committee investigating the Venezuela-British Guiana boundary dispute and then served as the American representative to the Tribunal that settled the dispute.[3]

NOTED OPINIONS

Although modern commentators classify Brewer as a product of his age and undistinguished in his work, some of his opinions confronted accepted standards and a few transcended his times. Modern judgment on Brewer is a reflection of how far out of step we are from Brewer's time and our history. Treatment of Brewer's opinion in *Church of the Holy Trinity* is instructive. The standard biography of Supreme Court Justices devotes 34 pages to Brewer but fails to mention this important decision.[4] By contrast, the eulogy delivered by the Attorney General of the United States devotes more time to *Church of the Holy Trinity* than any other case and mentions Brewer's opinion in it as first among his works.[5]

The necessity of protecting private property was a frequent theme of Brewer's speeches and articles. In 1886, he was the lone voice arguing that government regulations severely limiting the use of private property was a "taking," for which the government should compensate the owner. Only in 1992 did the U.S. Supreme Court finally accept such a proposition.[6]

Brewer's opinion in *Mueller v. State of Oregon* was also important. *Mueller* involved an Oregon statute limiting work days for women to ten hours. The Court had previously struck down a state law limiting bakers to ten hours a day as a violation of the bakers' freedom to contract. Speaking for a unanimous court, Brewer crafted an opinion distinguishing the baker decision and upholding the Oregon statute. He recognized the necessity of individual freedom and the right of women to equal personal and contractual freedom, but he also recognized that differences in women's physical structure and "maternal functions" prohibited their "full assertion of those rights." This difference justified legislation to secure a "real quality of rights." By recognizing a God-created difference between the sexes, Brewer avoided the two extremes of prohibiting all protective legislation and legislating equality in spite of physical differences.

Mueller and *Holy Trinity* both suggested principled resolutions to seemingly irreconcilable conflicts. Both decisions demonstrated that Brewer applied his work as Supreme Court Justice towards the hope of a biblically-informed Court.

NOTES

1. 218 *United States Reports* at xvi (1911).

2. Leon Friedman and Frank L. Israel, *The Justices of the United States Supreme Court 1789–1969* (New York: Chelsea House, 1969), 2:1520.

3. Friedman and Israel, *Justices of the United States Supreme Court,* 2:1522.

4. Friedman and Israel, *The Justices of the United States Supreme Court.*

5. 218 *United States Reports* at ix.

6. *Lucas v. South Carolina Coastal Council,* 503 US 1003 (1992).

LECTURE 1

The United States A Christian Nation

The signing of the Mayflower Compact:"…having undertaken for the glory of God and the advancement of the Christian faith…"

LECTURE 1

The United States A Christian Nation

WE CLASSIFY NATIONS IN VARIOUS WAYS. AS, FOR INSTANCE, by their form of government. One is a kingdom, another an empire, and still another a republic. Also by race. Great Britain is an Anglo-Saxon nation, France a Gallic, Germany a Teutonic, Russia a Slav. And still again by religion. One is a Mohammedan nation, others are heathen, and still others are Christian nations.

This republic is classified among the Christian nations of the world. It was so formally declared by the Supreme Court of the United States. In the case of *Holy Trinity Church vs. United States,* 143 U.S. 471, that court, after mentioning various circumstances, added, "these and many other matters which might be noticed, add a volume of unofficial declarations to the mass of organic utterances that this is a Christian nation."

But in what sense can it be called a Christian nation? Not in the sense that Christianity is the established religion or that the people are in any manner compelled to support it. On the contrary, the Constitution specifically provides that "Congress shall make no law respecting an establishment of religion, or prohibiting the free exercise thereof." Neither is it Christian in the sense that all its citizens are either in fact or name Christians. On the contrary, all religions have free scope within our borders. Numbers of our people profess other religions, and many reject all. Nor is it Christian in the sense that a profession of Christianity is a condition of holding office or otherwise engaging in the public service, or essential to recognition either politically or socially. In fact, the government as a legal organization is independent of all religions.

Nevertheless, we constantly speak of this republic as a Christian nation—in fact, as the leading Christian nation of the world.

This popular use of the term certainly has significance. It is not a mere creation of the imagination. It is not a term of derision but has a substantial basis—one which justifies its use. Let us analyze a little and see what is the basis.

EARLY SETTLEMENTS

The use of the term "Christian nation" has had from the early settlements on our shores and still has an official foundation. It is only about three centuries since the beginnings of civilized life within the limits of these United States. And those beginnings were in a marked and marvelous degree identified with Christianity. The commission from Ferdinand and Isabella to Columbus recites that "it is hoped that by God's assistance some of the continents and islands in the ocean will be discovered." The first colonial grant, that was made to Sir Walter Raleigh, in 1584, authorized him to enact statutes for the government of the proposed colony, provided that "they be not against the true Christian faith now professed in the Church of England."

COLONIAL CHARTERS

The first charter of Virginia, granted by King James I, in 1606, after reciting the application of certain parties for a charter, commenced the grant in these words: "We, greatly commending, and graciously accepting of, their desires for the furtherance of so noble a work, which may, by the providence of Almighty God, hereafter tend to the glory of His Divine Majesty, in propagating the Christian religion to such people as yet live in darkness and miserable ignorance of the true knowledge and worship of God." And language of similar import is found in subsequent charters of the same colony, from the same king, in 1609 and 1611. The celebrated compact made by the Pilgrims on the *Mayflower,* in 1620, recites: "Having undertaken for the glory of God and advancement of the Christian faith and the honor of our king and country a voyage to plant the first colony in the northern parts of Virginia."

The charter of New England, granted by James I in 1620, after referring to a petition, declares: "We, according to our princely inclination, favoring much their worthy disposition, in hope thereby to advance the enlargement of Christian religion, to the glory of God Almighty."

The charter of Massachusetts Bay, granted in 1629 by Charles I, after several provisions, recites: "Whereby our said people, inhabitants there, may be so religiously, peaceably and civilly governed as their good life and orderly conversation may win and incite the natives of the country to their knowledge and obedience of the only true God and Saviour of mankind, and the Christian faith, which in our royal intention and the adventurers free profession, is the principal end of this plantation," which declaration was substantially repeated in the charter of Massachusetts Bay granted by William and Mary, in 1691.

The fundamental orders of Connecticut, under which a provisional government was instituted in 1638 - 1639, provided:

> Forasmuch as it has pleased the Almighty God by the wise disposition of His divine providence so to order and dispose of things that we, the inhabitants and residents of Windsor, Hartford and Wethersfield, are now cohabitating and dwelling in and upon the River of Connecticut and the lands thereto adjoining; and well knowing where a people are gathered together the word of God requires that to maintain the peace and union of such a people there should be an orderly and decent government established according to God, to order and dispose of the affairs of the people at all seasons as occasion shall require; do therefore associate and conjoin ourselves to be as one public state or commonwealth; and do for ourselves and our successors and such as shall be adjoined to us at any time hereafter enter into combination and confederation together to maintain and preserve the liberty and purity of the gospel of our Lord Jesus which we now profess, as also the discipline of the churches, which, according to the truth of the said gospel, is now practiced amongst us.

In the preamble of the Constitution of 1776 it is declared, "the free fruition of such liberties and privileges as humanity, civility and Christianity call for, as is due to every man in his place and proportion, without impeachment and infringement, hath ever been, and will be the tran-

15

quility and stability of churches and commonwealths; and the denial thereof, the disturbance, if not the ruin of both."

In 1638 the first settlers in Rhode Island organized a local government by signing the following agreement:

> We whose names are underwritten do here solemnly in the presence of Jehovah incorporate ourselves into a Bodie Politick and as He shall help, will submit our persons, lives and estates unto our Lord Jesus Christ, the King of Kings and Lord of Lords and to all those perfect and most absolute laws of his given us in his holy word of truth, to be guided and judged thereby. *EXOD. 24: 3, 4; II CHRON. 11:3; II KINGS.*

The charter granted to Rhode Island, in 1663, naming the petitioners, speaks of them as "pursuing, with peaceable and loyal minds, their sober, serious and religious intentions, of godly edifying themselves and one another in the holy Christian faith and worship as they were persuaded; together with the gaining over and conversion of the poor, ignorant Indian natives, in these parts of America, to the sincere profession and obedience of the same faith and worship."

The charter of Carolina, granted in 1663 by Charles II, recites that the petitioners, "being excited with a laudable and pious zeal for the propagation of the Christian faith." In the preface of the frame of government prepared in 1682 by William Penn, for Pennsylvania, it is said: "They weakly err, that think there is no other use of government than correction, which is the coarsest part of it; daily experience tells us that the care and regulation of many other affairs, more soft, and daily necessary, make up much of the greatest part of government; and which must have followed the peopling of the world, had Adam never fell, and will continue among men, on earth, under the highest attainments they may arrive at, by the coming of the blessed second Adam, "the Lord from heaven." And with the laws prepared to go with the frame of government, it was further provided "that according to the good example of the primitive Christians, and the ease of the creation, every first day of the week, called the Lord's Day, people shall abstain from their common daily labor that they may the better dispose themselves to worship God according to their understandings."

In the charter of privileges granted, in 1701, by William Penn to the province of Pennsylvania and territories thereunto belonging (such territories afterwards constituting the State of Delaware), it is recited: "Because no people can be truly happy, though under the greatest enjoyment of civil liberties, if abridged of the freedom of their consciences as to their religious profession and worship; and Almighty God being the only Lord of Conscience, Father of Lights and Spirits, and the author as well as object of all divine knowledge, faith and worship, who only doth enlighten the minds and persuade and convince the understandings of the people, I do hereby grant and declare." The Constitution of Vermont, of 1777, granting the free exercise of religious worship, added, "Nevertheless, every sect or denomination of people ought to observe the Sabbath, or the Lord's day, and keep up and support some sort of religious worship, which to them shall seem most agreeable to the revealed will of God." And this was repeated in the Constitution of 1786.

COLONIAL CONSTITUTIONS

In the Constitution of South Carolina, of 1778, it was declared that "the Christian Protestant religion shall be deemed and is hereby constituted and declared to be the established religion of this State." And further, that no agreement or union of men upon pretense of religion should be entitled to become incorporated and regarded as a church of the established religion of the State, without agreeing and subscribing to a book of five articles, the third and fourth of which were "that the Christian religion is the true religion; that the holy scriptures of the Old and New Testament are of divine inspiration, and are the rule of faith and practice."

Passing beyond these declarations which are found in the organic instruments of the colonies, the following are well known historical facts: Lord Baltimore secured the charter for a Maryland colony in order that he and his associates might continue their Catholic worship free from Protestant persecution. Roger Williams, exiled from Massachusetts because of his religious views, established an independent colony in Rhode Island.

The Huguenots, driven from France by the Edict of Nantes, sought in the more southern colonies a place where they could live in the enjoyment of their Huguenot faith. It is not exaggeration to say that Christianity in some of its creeds was the principal cause of the settlement of many of the colonies, and cooperated with business hopes and purposes in the settlement of the others. Beginning in this way and under these influences it is not strange that the colonial life had an emphatic Christian tone.

From the very first, efforts were made, largely it must be conceded by Catholics, to bring the Indians under the influence of Christianity. Who can read without emotion the story of Marquette, and others like him, enduring all perils and dangers and toiling through the forests of the west in their efforts to tell the story of Jesus to the savages of North America?

Within less than one hundred years from the landing at Jamestown three colleges were established in the colonies; Harvard in Massachusetts, William and Mary in Virginia and Yale in Connecticut. The first seal used by Harvard College had as a motto, "In Christi Gloriam," and the charter granted by Massachusetts Bay contained this recital: "Whereas, through the good hand of God many well devoted persons have been and daily are moved and stirred up to give and bestow sundry gifts...that may conduce to the education of the English and Indian youth of this country, in knowledge and godliness." The charter of William and Mary, reciting that the proposal was "to the end that the Church of Virginia may be furnished with a seminary of ministers of the gospel, and that the youth may be piously educated in good letters and manners, and that the Christian faith may be propagated amongst the western Indians, to the glory of Almighty God" made the grant "for propagating the pure gospel of Christ, our only Mediator, to the praise and honor of Almighty God." The charter of Yale declared as its purpose to fit "young men for public employment both in church and civil state," and it provided that the trustees should be Congregational ministers living in the colony.

In some of the colonies, particularly in New England, the support of the church was a matter of public charge, even as the common schools are to-day. Thus the Constitution of Massachusetts, of 1780, Part I, Article 3, provided that "the legislature shall, from time to time, authorize and require, the several towns, parishes, precincts, and other bodies politic or religious societies to make suitable provision at their own expense for the institution of the public worship of God and for the support and maintenance of Protestant teachers of piety, religion and morality in all cases where such provision shall not be made voluntarily."

Article 6 of the Bill of Rights of the Constitution of New Hampshire, of 1784, repeated in the Constitution of 1784, empowered "the legislature to authorize from time to time, the several towns, parishes, bodies corporate, or religious societies within this State, to make adequate provision at their own expense for the support and maintenance of public Protestant teachers of piety, religion and morality." In the fundamental Constitutions of 1769, prepared for the Carolinas, by the celebrated John Locke, Article 96 reads: "As the country comes to be sufficiently planted and distributed into fit divisions, it shall belong to the parliament to take care for the building of churches, and the public maintenance of divines to be employed in the exercise of religion according to the Church of England, which being the only true and orthodox and the national religion of all the king's dominions, is so also of Carolina, and, therefore, it alone shall be allowed to receive public maintenance by grant of parliament."

In Maryland, by the Constitution of 1776, it was provided that "the legislature may, in their discretion, lay a general and equal tax, for the support of the Christian religion."

In several colonies and states a profession of the Christian faith was made an indispensable condition to holding office. In the frame of government for Pennsylvania, prepared by William Penn, in 1683, it was provided that "all treasurers, judges...and other officers...and all members elected to serve in provincial council and general assembly, and all that have right to elect such members, shall be such as profess faith in Jesus Christ." And in the charter of privileges for that colony, given in 1701 by William Penn and approved by the colonial assembly, it was provided "that all persons who also profess to believe in Jesus Christ, the Saviour of the world, shall be capable...to serve this government in any capacity, both legislatively and executively."

In Delaware, by the Constitution of 1776, every officeholder was required to make and subscribe the following declaration: "I, A. B., do profess faith in God the Father, and in Jesus Christ His Only Son, and in the Holy Ghost, one God, blessed forevermore; and I do acknowledge the Holy Scriptures of the Old and New Testament to be given by divine inspiration."

New Hampshire, in the Constitutions of 1784 and 1792, required that senators and representatives should be of the "Protestant religion," and this provision remained in force until 1877.

The fundamental Constitutions of the Carolinas declared: "No man shall be permitted to be a freeman of Carolina, or to have any estate or habitation within it that doth not acknowledge a God, and that God is publicly and solemnly to be worshiped."

The Constitution of North Carolina, of 1776, provided: "That no person who shall deny the being of God or the truth of the Protestant religion, or the divine authority either of the Old or New Testaments, or who shall hold religious principles incompatible with the freedom and safety of the State, shall be capable of holding any office or place of trust or profit in the civil department within this State." And this remained in force until 1835, when it was amended by changing the word "Protestant" to "Christian," and as so amended remained in force until the Constitution of 1868. And in that Constitution among the persons disqualified for office were "all persons who shall deny the being of Almighty God."

New Jersey, by the Constitution of 1776, declared "that no Protestant inhabitant of this colony shall be denied the enjoyment of any civil right merely on account of his religious principles, but that all persons professing a belief in the faith of any Protestant sect, who shall demean themselves peaceably under the government as hereby established, shall be capable of being elected into any office of profit or trust, or being a member of either branch of the legislature."

The Constitution of South Carolina, of 1776, provided that no person should be eligible to the Senate or House of Representatives "unless he be of the Protestant religion."

Massachusetts, in its Constitution of 1780, required from governor, lieutenant-governor, councillor, senator and representative before proceeding to execute the duties of his place or office a declaration that "I believe the Christian religion, and have a firm persuasion of its truth."

By the fundamental orders of Connecticut the governor was directed to take an oath to "further the execution of justice according to the rule of God's word; so help me God, in the name of the Lord Jesus Christ."

The Vermont Constitution of 1777 required of every member of the House of Representatives that he take this oath: "I do believe in one God, the creator and governor of the universe, the rewarder of the good and punisher of the wicked, and I do acknowledge the scriptures of the Old and New Testaments to be given by divine inspiration, and own and profess the Protestant religion." A similar requirement was provided by the Constitution of 1786.

In Maryland, by the Constitution of 1776, every person appointed to any office of profit or trust was not only to take an official oath of allegiance to the State, but also to "subscribe a declaration of his belief in the Christian religion." In the same State, in the Constitution of 1851, it was declared that no other test or qualification for admission to any office of trust or profit shall be required than the official oath "and a declaration of belief in the Christian religion; and if the party shall profess to be a Jew the declaration shall be of his belief in a future state of rewards and punishments." As late as 1864 the same State in its Constitution had a similar provision, the change being one merely of phraseology, the provision reading, "a declaration of belief in the Christian religion, or of the existence of God, and in a future state of rewards and punishments."

Mississippi, by the Constitution of 1817, provided that "no person who denies the being of God or a future state of rewards and punishments shall hold any office in the civil department of the State."

THE RECOGNITION OF SUNDAY

Another significant matter is the recognition of Sunday. That day is the Christian Sabbath, a day peculiar to that faith, and known to no other. It would be impossible within the limits of a lecture to point out all the ways in which that day is recognized.

The following illustrations must suffice: By the United States Constitution the President is required to approve all bills passed by Congress. If he disapproves he returns it with his veto. And then specifically it is provided that if not returned by him within ten days, "Sundays excepted," after it shall have been presented to him it becomes a law. Similar provisions are found in the Constitutions of most of the States, and in thirty-six out of forty-five is the same expression, "Sundays excepted." Louisiana is one of the nine States in whose present Constitution the expression, "Sundays excepted," is not found. Four earlier Constitutions of that State (those of 1812, 1845, 1852 and 1864) contained, while the three later ones, 1868, 1879 and 1881 omit those words. In State ex rel. vs. Secretary of State, a case arising under the last Constitution, decided by the Supreme Court of Louisiana (52 La. An. 936), the question was presented as to the effect of a governor's veto which was returned within time if a Sunday intervening between the day of presentation of the bill and the return of the veto was excluded, and too late if it was included; the burden of the contention on the one side being that the change in the phraseology of the later Constitutions in omitting the words "Sundays excepted" indicated a change in the meaning of the constitutional provision in respect to the time of a veto. The court unanimously held that the Sunday was to be excluded. In the course of its opinion it said (p. 944):

> In law Sundays are generally excluded as days upon which the performance of any act demanded by the law is not required. They are held to be *dies non juridici*.
> And in the Christian world Sunday is regarded as the "Lord's Day," and a holiday—a day of cessation from labor.
> By statute, enacted as far back as 1838, this day is made in Louisiana one of "public rest." Rev. Stat., Sec. 522; Code of Practice, 207, 763.
> This is the policy of the State of long standing and the framers of the Constitution are to be considered as intending to conform to the same.

By express command of Congress, studies are not pursued at the military or naval academies, and distilleries are prohibited from operation on Sundays, while chaplains are required to hold religious services once at least on that day.

By the English statute of Charles II no tradesman, artificer, workman, laborer, or other person was permitted to do or exercise any worldly labor, business or work of ordinary calling upon the Lord's Day, or any part thereof, works of necessity or charity only excepted. That statute, with some variations, has been adopted by most if not all the States of the Union. In Massachusetts it was held that one injured while traveling in the cars on Sunday, except in case of necessity or charity, was guilty of contributory negligence and could recover nothing from the railroad company for the injury he sustained. And this decision was affirmed by the Supreme Court of the United States. A statute of the State of Georgia, making the running of freight trains on Sunday a misdemeanor, was also upheld by that court. By decisions in many States a contract made on Sunday is invalid and cannot be enforced. By the general course of decision no judicial proceedings can be held on Sunday. All legislative bodies, whether municipal, state or national, abstain from work on that day. Indeed, the vast volume of official action, legislative and judicial, recognizes Sunday as a day separate and apart from the others, a day devoted not to the ordinary pursuits of life. It is true in many of the decisions this separation of the day is said to be authorized by the police power of the State and exercised for purposes of health. At the same time, through a large majority of them, there runs the thought of its being a religious day, consecrated by the Commandment, "Six days shalt thou labor, and do all thy work: but the seventh day is the Sabbath of the Lord thy God: in it thou shalt not do any work, thou, nor thy son, nor thy daughter, thy man servant, nor thy maid servant, nor thy cattle, nor the stranger that is within thy gates."

THE NAME OF GOD

While the word "God" is not infrequently used both in the singular and plural to denote any supreme being or beings, yet when used alone and in the singular number it generally refers to that Supreme Being spoken of in the Old and New Testaments and worshiped by Jew and Christian. In that sense the word is used in constitution, statute and instrument. In many State Constitutions we find in the preamble a declaration like this: "Grateful to Almighty God." In some he who denied the being of God was disqualified from holding office. It is again and again declared in constitution and statute that official oaths shall close with an appeal, "So help me, God." When, upon inauguration, the President-elect each four years consecrates himself to the great responsibilities of Chief Executive of the republic, his vow of consecration in the presence of the vast throng filling the Capitol grounds will end with the solemn words, "So help me, God." In all our courts witnesses in like manner vouch for the truthfulness of their testimony. The common commencement of wills is "In the name of God, Amen." Every foreigner attests his renunciation of allegiance to his former sovereign and his acceptance of citizenship in this republic by an appeal to God.

These various declarations in charters, constitutions and statutes indicate the general thought and purpose. If it be said that similar declarations are not found in all the charters or in all the constitutions, it will be borne in mind that the omission oftentimes was because they were deemed unnecessary, as shown by the quotation just made from the opinion of the Supreme Court of Louisiana, as well as those hereafter taken from the opinions of other courts. And further, it is of still more significance that there are no contrary declarations. In no charter or constitution is there anything to even suggest that any other than the Christian is the religion of this country. In none of them is Mohammed or Confucius or Buddha in any manner noticed. In none of them is Judaism recognized other than by way of toleration of its special creed. While the separation of church and state is often affirmed, there is nowhere a repudiation of Christianity as one of the institutions as well as benedictions of society. In short, there is no charter or constitution that is either infidel, agnostic or anti-Christian. Wherever there is a declaration in favor of any religion it is of the Christian. In view of the multitude of expressions in its favor, the avowed separation between church and state is a most satisfactory testimonial that it is the religion of this country, for a peculiar thought of Christianity is of a personal relation between man and his Maker, uncontrolled by and independent of human government.

CHAPLAINS

Notice also the matter of chaplains. These are appointed for the army and navy, named as officials of legislative assemblies, and universally they belong to one or other of the Christian denominations. Their whole range of service, whether in prayer or preaching, is an official recognition of Christianity. If it be not so, why do we have chaplains?

DECLARATIONS OF THE COURTS

If we consult the decisions of the courts, although the formal question has seldom been presented because of a general recognition of its truth, yet in *The People vs. Ruggles*, 8 John. 290, 294, 295, Chancellor Kent, the great commentator on American law, speaking as Chief Justice of the Supreme Court of New York, said: "The people of this State, in common with the people of this country, profess the general doctrines of Christianity, as the rule of their faith and practice." And in the famous case of *Vidal vs. Girard's Executors*, 2 How. 127, 198, the Supreme Court of the United States, while sustaining the will of Mr. Girard, with its provision for the creation of a college into which no minister should be permitted to enter, observed: "It is also said, and truly, that the Christian religion is a part of the common law of Pennsylvania."

The New York Supreme Court, in *Lindenmuller vs. The People*, 33 Barbour, 561, held that:

> Christianity is not the legal religion of the State, as established by law. If it were, it would be a civil or political institution, which it is not; but this is not inconsistent with the idea that it is in fact, and ever has been, the religion of the people. This fact is everywhere prominent in all our civil and political history, and has been, from the first, recognized and acted upon by the people, as well as by constitutional conventions, by legislatures and by courts of justice.

The South Carolina Supreme Court, in *State vs. Chandler*, 2 Harrington, 555, citing many cases, said:

> It appears to have been long perfectly settled by the common law that

blasphemy against the Deity in general, or a malicious and wanton attack against the Christian religion individually, for the purpose of exposing its doctrines to contempt and ridicule, is indictable and punishable as a temporal offense.

And again, in *City Council vs. Benjamin,* 2 Strobhart, 521:

On that day we rest, and to us it is the Sabbath of the Lord—its decent observance in a Christian community is that which ought to be expected.

It is not perhaps necessary for the purposes of this case to rule and hold that the Christian religion is part of the common law of South Carolina. Still it may be useful to show that it lies at the foundation of even the article of the Constitution under consideration, and that upon it rest many of the principles and usages, constantly acknowledged and enforced, in the courts of justice.

The Pennsylvania Supreme Court, in *Updegraph vs. The Commonwealth,* 11 Sergeant and Rawle, 400, made this declaration:

Christianity, general Christianity, is, and always has been, a part of the common law of Pennsylvania; Christianity, without the spiritual artillery of European countries; for this Christianity was one of the considerations of the royal charter, and the very basis of its great founder, William Penn; not Christianity founded on any particular religious tenets; not Christianity with an established church, and tithes, and spiritual courts; but Christianity with liberty of conscience to all men.

And subsequently, in *Johnson vs. The Commonwealth,* 10 Harris, 111:

"It is not our business to discuss the obligations of Sunday any further than they enter into and are recognized by the law of the land. The common law adopted it, along with Christianity, of which it is one of the bulwarks."

In Arkansas, *Shover vs. The State,* 10 English, 263, the Supreme Court said:

Sunday or the Sabbath is properly and emphatically called the Lord's Day, and is one amongst the first and most sacred institutions of the Christian religion. This system of religion is recognized as constituting a part and parcel of the common law, and as such all of the institutions growing out of it, or, in any way, connected with it, in case they shall not be found to interfere with the rights of conscience, are entitled to the most profound respect, and can rightfully claim the protection of the law-making power of the State.

The Supreme Court of Maryland, in *Judefind vs. The State,* 78 Maryland, 514, declared:

The Sabbath is emphatically the day of rest, and the day of rest here is the Lord's Day or Christian's Sunday. Ours is a Christian community, and a day set apart as the day of rest is the day consecrated by the resurrection of our Saviour, and embraces the twenty-four hours next ensuing the midnight of Saturday. But it would scarcely be asked of a court, in what professes to be a Christian land, to declare a law unconstitutional because it requires rest from bodily labor on Sunday (except works of necessity and charity) and thereby promotes the cause of Christianity.

UNOFFICIAL DECLARATIONS

If now we pass from the domain of official action and recognition to that of individual acceptance we enter a field of boundless extent, and I can only point out a few of the prominent facts:

Notice our educational institutions. I have already called your attention to the provisions of the charters of the first three colleges. Think of the vast number of academies, colleges and universities scattered through the land. Some of them, it is true, are under secular control, but there is yet to be established in this country one of those institutions founded on the religions of Confucius, Buddha or Mohammed, while an overwhelming majority are under the special direction and control of Christian teachers.

Notice also the avowed and pronounced Christian forces of the country, and here I must refer to the census of 1890, for the statistics of the census of 1900 in these matters have not been compiled: The population was 62,622,000. There were 165,000 Christian church organizations, owning 142,000 buildings, in which were sittings for 40,625,000 people. The communicants in these churches numbered 20,476,000, and the value of the church property amounted to $669,876,000. In other words, about one-third of the entire population were directly connected with Christian organizations.

Nearly two-thirds would find seats in our churches. If to the members we add the children and others in their families more or less connected with them, it is obvious that a large majority were attached to the various church organizations. I am aware that the relationship between many members and their churches is formal, and that church relations do not constitute active and paramount forces in their lives, and yet it is clear that there is an identification of the great mass of American citizens with the Christian church. It is undoubtedly true that there is no little complaint of the falling off in church attendance, and of a lukewarmness on the part of many, and on the other hand there is a diversion of religious force along the lines of the Young Men's Christian Association, the Christian Endeavor Society and the Epworth League. All these, of course, are matters to be noticed, but they do not avoid the fact of a formal adhesion of the great majority of our people to the Christian faith; and while creeds and dogmas and denominations are in a certain sense losing their power, and certainly their antagonisms, yet as a vital force in the land, Christianity is still the mighty factor. Connected with the denominations are large missionary bodies constantly busy in extending Christian faith through this nation and through the world. No other religious organization has anything of a foothold or is engaged in active work unless it be upon so small a scale as scarcely to be noticed in the great volume of American life.

Again, the Bible is the Christian's book. No other book has so wide a circulation, or is so universally found in the households of the land. During their century of existence the English and American Bible Societies have published and circulated two hundred and fifty million copies, and this represents but a fraction of its circulation. And then think of the multitude of volumes published in exposition, explanation and illustration of that book, or some portion of it.

No Doubtful Facts

You will have noticed that I have presented no doubtful facts. Nothing has been stated which is debatable. The quotations from charters are in the archives of the several States; the laws are on the statute books; judicial opinions are taken from the official reports; statistics from the census publications. In short, no evidence has been presented which is open to question.

I could easily enter upon another line of examination. I could point out the general trend of public opinion, the disclosures of purposes and beliefs to be found in letters, papers, books and unofficial declarations. I could show how largely our laws and customs are based upon the laws of Moses and the teachings of Christ; how constantly the Bible is appealed to as the guide of life and the authority in questions of morals: how the Christian doctrines are accepted as the great comfort in times of sorrow and affliction, and fill with the light of hope the services for the dead. On every hilltop towers the steeple of some Christian church, while from the marble witnesses in God's acre comes the universal but silent testimony to the common faith in the Christian doctrine of the resurrection and the life hereafter.

But I must not weary you. I could go on indefinitely, pointing out further illustrations both official and non-official, public and private; such as the annual Thanksgiving proclamations, with their following days of worship and feasting; announcements of days of fasting and prayer; the universal celebration of Christmas; the gathering of millions of our children in Sunday Schools, and the countless volumes of Christian literature, both prose and poetry. But I have said enough to show that Christianity came to this country with the first colonists; has been powerfully identified with its rapid development, colonial and national, and to-day exists as a mighty factor in the life of the republic. This is a Christian nation, and we can all rejoice as truthfully we repeat the words of Leonard Bacon:

> *O God, beneath thy guiding hand*
> *Our exiled fathers crossed the sea,*
> *And when they trod the wintry strand,*
> *With prayer and psalm they worshiped Thee.*
>
> *Thou heardst, well pleased, the song, the prayer—*
> *Thy blessing came; and still its power*
> *Shall onward through all ages bear*
> *The memory of that holy hour.*
>
> *Laws, freedom, truth, and faith in God*
> *Came with those exiles o'er the waves,*
> *And where their pilgrim feet have trod,*
> *The God they trusted guards their graves.*
>
> *And here Thy name, O God of love,*
> *Their children's children shall adore,*
> *Till these eternal hills remove,*
> *And spring adorns the earth no more.*

LECTURE II

Our Duty as Citizens

Prayer opened the first session of the Continental Congress—and every session since.

LECTURE II

Our Duty as Citizens

I CONSIDERED LAST NIGHT THE PROPOSITION THAT THE UNITED States of America is a Christian nation. I pointed out that Christianity was a primary cause of the first settlement on our shores; that the organic instruments, charters and constitutions of the colonies were filled with abundant recognitions of it as a controlling factor in the life of the people; that in one at least of them it was in terms declared the established religion, while in several the furthering of Christianity was stated to be one of the purposes of the government; in many faith in it was a condition of holding office; in some, authority was given to the legislature to make its support a public charge; in nearly all the constitutions there has been an express recognition of the sanctity of the Christian Sunday; the God of the Bible is appealed to again and again. Sunday laws have been enacted and enforced in most of the colonies and States. About one-third of the population are avowedly Christian and communicants in some Christian organization; there are sitting accommodations in the churches for nearly two-thirds; educational institutions are largely under the control of Christian denominations, and even in those which, in obedience to the rule of separation between church and state, are secular in their organization, the principles of Christianity are uniformly recognized. By these and other evidences I claim to have shown that the calling of this republic a Christian nation is not a mere pretence but a recognition of an historical, legal and social truth.

CITIZENS OF HEAVEN AND EARTH

I come this evening to consider the consequences of this fact and the duties it imposes upon all our citizens.

And first let it be noticed that there is no incompatibility between

Christianity and patriotism. The declaration of the Master, "Render therefore unto Caesar, the things which are Caesar's; and unto God, the things that are God's," is not a declaration of antagonism between the two, but an affirmation of duty to each. Indeed, devotion to one generally goes hand in hand with loyalty to the other. When Havelock, the hero of Lucknow, died, most appropriate were the words of the English poet:

> *Strew not on the hero's hearse*
> *Garlands of a herald's verse:*
> *Let us hear no words of Fame*
> *Sounding loud a deathless name:*
> *Tell us of no vauntful Glory*
> *Shouting forth her haughty story.*
> *All life long his homage rose*
> *To far other shrine than those.*
> *"In hoc signo," pale nor dim,*
> *Lit the battlefield for him,*
> *And the prize he sought and won,*
> *Was the crown for duty done.*

But we need not go elsewhere. In our own land, from the very first, Christianity and patriotism have worked together. When the Pilgrim Fathers touched New England's shores, their first service was one of thanksgiving and praise to that Infinite One who had, as they believed, guided them to their new home. In the long struggles of the early colonists with their Indian foes, the building on the hill was both church and fort. They fell on their knees and then on the aborigines, was the old satire, to which now is added, they fall on the Chinese. In the convention that framed the Constitution, when doubt and uncertainty hovered over the result, at Franklin's insistence prayer was offered for the success of their efforts. In the dark days at Valley Forge the great leader sought strength and inspiration in prayer. When the nation stood aghast at the assassination of Abraham Lincoln, the clarion voice of Garfield rang out above the darkness and the tumult, "God reigns, and the government at Washington still lives." And so I might go on with illustration after illustration showing how the faith of the Christian has stood in times of trial and trouble as the rock upon which the nation has rested.

CHRISTIANITY ON TRIAL

Again, Christianity is entitled to the tribute of respect. I do not of course mean that all individuals, nominally Christian, deserve trust, confidence, or even respect, for the contrary is too often the case. Too often men hold religion as they do property, in their wives' names. Nor is Christianity beyond the reach of criticism and opposition. It is not lifted up as something too sacred to be spoken of save in terms and tones of reverence.

This is an iconoclastic and scientific age. We are destroying many beliefs and traditions. William Tell is a myth. The long hairs of Pocahontas never dropped in protecting folds over the body of John Smith. The Arabs never destroyed the great library at Alexandria, though if some wandering Arabs would destroy all the law books in the land they would bless the courts and help the cause of justice. We challenge the truthfulness of every assertion of fact, every demand upon our faith and confidence; and Christianity must stand like all other institutions, to be challenged, criticized, weighed and its merits and demerits determined. The time has passed in the history of the world when anything is too sacred to be touched, when anything is beyond the reach of the inquiring and scientific sphere.

But while conceding all this, I insist that Christianity has been so wrought into the history of this republic, so identified with its growth and prosperity, has been and is so dear to the hearts of the great body of our citizens, that it ought not to be spoken of contemptuously or treated with ridicule. Religion of any form is a sacred matter. It involves the relation of the individual to some Being believed to be infinitely supreme. It involves not merely character and life here, but destiny hereafter, and as such is not to be spoken of lightly or flippantly. And we who are citizens of this republic — recognizing the identification of Christianity with its life, the general belief that Christianity is the best of all religions, that it passed into the lives of our fathers and is taken into the lives of our brethren as something of sacred power — ought, even if not agreeing with all that is claimed for it, to at least accord to it respect.

I once listened to a conversation which illustrates my thought. It was between two young men returning after the close of a summer's vacation to the college at which both were students. The principal talker was, as I discovered in the course of the afternoon, an only son. On his upper lip was the first dark shadow of a coming mustache. He possessed that peculiar wisdom which belongs in this world to only the college sophomore. He was expressing to his companion his views on the Bible and religion, said he knew too much to believe in either; admitted that his mother believed in both and read her Bible every day; said that that might do for women and children, but not for any intelligent man in the light of present scientific knowledge.

You would have thought that Darwin and Huxley and Lord Kelvin had studied at his feet and that he was the Gamaliel of the present day. It is impossible to reproduce in language the self-sufficient sneering tone in which he spoke of the Bible, classing it with nursery rhymes, the story of Jack and the Beanstalk and the like, and the complacent pity with which he referred to those who were foolish enough to regard it as a sacred book. It is to be hoped that the budding sophomore lived long enough to learn that no gentleman speaks sneeringly of that which has been the life-long faith and comfort of his mother.

SHE'S A GRAND OLD FLAG

From the standpoint of citizenship the treatment of Christianity may be regarded as in some respects similar to that which is accorded and is due to the national flag.

Who looks upon that as a mere piece of cloth costing but a trifle, something to be derided or trampled upon at will? A particular banner may not have cost much. It may be cheap to him who sees only the material and work which have passed into it, but to every patriot it is the symbol of patriotism. Its history is a record of glory. A century ago, the Barbary pirates, who had defied the flags of Europe, saw it waving over Decatur's vessels and bowed in submission. Commodore Perry sailed beneath it into the unknown harbors of Japan, opened that nation to the nineteenth century, and today her civilization and power command universal respect and admiration. The oppressed Cuban appealed to it for deliverance, and in response thereto Manila and Santiago de Cuba introduced a new sister into the family of nations.

> *Wherever man has dared to go,*
> *'Mid tropic heat or polar snow,*
> *On sandy plain or lofty crag,*
> *Has waved our country's starry flag.*
> *In that far North where ceaseless cold*
> *Has built its alabaster hold,*
> *And where the sun disdains to show*
> *His brightness on unbroken snow,*
> *Where icy pillars tower to heaven*
> *Pale sentinels to nature given,*
> *To watch the only spot she can*
> *Withhold from grasping hand of man,*
> *There Kane unfurled this banner bright,*
> *Resplendent with auroral light.*

Today the flag waves at the masthead of American vessels in every water of the globe, and commands the world's respect. An insult to it every citizen feels is an insult to himself, and all insist that it shall be accorded due respect. We remember how, in the early days of our great civil struggle, the loyal heart was stirred with the thrilling words of Secretary Dix, "If any man attempts to haul down the American flag, shoot him on the spot." We honor Stonewall Jackson, who, seeing Barbara Frietchie waving this banner from the window of her home in Frederick, and the threatening guns of his soldiers, called out:

> *"Who touches a hair of yon gray head*
> *Dies like a dog. March on;" he said.*

We rejoice that now it floats in peace and triumph over all our fair land. We love to watch its folds swing out to the breeze on every patriotic day, to see it decorate the walls where gather our great conventions. We glory in every tribute that is paid to it in any part of the globe. It tells the story of conflicts, of defeats and victories. It has waved over many a field of battle, and the blood of our noblest and best has been shed in its defense. It is eloquent of all the sufferings and trials of days gone by, of all the great achievements of the American people, and as we swing it to the breeze we do so with undoubting faith that it will wave over grander things in the future of this republic.

SHE'S A GRAND OLD FAITH

Christianity has entered into and become part of the life of this republic; it came with its beginnings and prompted them; has been identified with its toils and trials, shared in its victories, cheered in the hour of darkness and gloom, and stands today prophetic of untold blessings in the future. And shall it be said that it alone of all our benedictions has forfeited a claim to receive from every American citizen the tribute of respect?

Respect for Christianity implies respectful treatment of its institutions and ordinances. This does not require that every one must conform his life to those institutions and ordinances. That is something which each one has a right to settle for himself. Take, for instance, the matter of church services. No one is in duty bound as a citizen to attend a particular church service, or indeed any church service. The freedom of conscience, the liberty of the individual, gives to every individual the right to attend or stay away.

At the same time, there is an obligation not to unnecessarily interfere with or disturb those services. This is something more than the duty which rests upon one attending those services to avoid the ungentlemanly and unseemly act of disturbing the exercises. That is only a part of the common courtesy of all going into a gathering assembled for any lawful purpose. They who call the meeting and who are engaged in service of any legitimate character have a right to be free from annoyance and interference. But, even beyond that, the citizen who does not attend, does not even share in the belief of those who do, ought ever to bear in mind the noble part Christianity has taken in the history of the republic, the great share it has had in her wonderful development and its contribution to her present glory, and by reason thereof take pains to secure to those who do believe in it and do attend its services freedom from all disturbance of their peaceful gathering. The American Christian is entitled to his quiet hour.

REMEMBER THE SABBATH DAY

Take another illustration — Sunday. Its separation from the other days as a day of rest is enforced by the legislation of nearly all if not all the States of the Union. Beyond that, it is to the Christian a sacred day. It does not follow that it is the duty of every individual to observe the Sabbath as Christians do. Indeed, there is no unanimity of view among the latter as to the manner in which it should be observed. We have gone far away from the Puritan Sabbath and the austere, severe observance of it which prevailed in the early days of New England colonies, and which made the day a terror to children as well as burdensome to adults. I believe it is conceded that notwithstanding the fabled blue laws of New England, a man may without impropriety kiss his wife on Sunday and possibly if he has a chance some other sweet-faced woman. That old-time terror has been superseded by gentler and kindlier modes of observance, which tend to make the day welcome to all, both young and old, one in which is not merely rest from the ordinary toils of the week, but one in which the companionship of friends, the sweet influences of nature, and lessons from the higher forms of music and other arts are recognized as among its benedictions.

While the latter modes, though very likely more helpful, more really Christian, are a great departure from the former, yet it still remains true that it is a day consecrated of old, a day separated by law and religion as well as by the custom of the church for ages, and ought not to be turned into a day of public frivolity and gaiety. While it may be true that all are not under obligations to conform to the higher and better uses of the day, yet at least they owe that respect to Christianity to pursue their frivolities and gaieties in such a way as not to offend those who believe in its sacredness. I recognize the fact that it is not always easy to draw the line and that freedom implies not merely the freedom of those who would keep the day sacred, but also the freedom of those who do not so regard it. Again, it deserves the attention and study of every citizen. You are all patriots, you love your country, are proud of its past and mean to so live and act that you can help it to the best possible future.

THE FAITH OF OUR FATHERS

Now, as I have pointed out, Christianity was a principal cause of the settlements on these western shores. It has been identified with the growth and development of those settlements into the United States of America, has so largely shaped and molded it that today of all the nations in the world it is the most justly called a Christian nation. In order to determine what we ought to do for the future of the republic we must review its history, inquire into the causes which have made its growth and influenced its life, ascertained which have been the most controlling and which have helped on the better side of its development, and why they have been so influential.

I have shown that Christianity has been a great factor, and the student of our history will find that it has been a helpful and uplifting factor. Making full allowance for all the imperfections and mistakes which have attended it, as they attend all human institutions, I am sure that the student will be convinced that its general influence upon our national life has been for the better.

HOME AND WORK

Christianity has always stood for purity of the home, and who doubts that our homes have been the centers of the holiest living. It is Mormonism, Mohammedanism, and heathenism and not Christianity which have proclaimed polygamy and debased woman from the sacred place of wife to the lower level of concubine. It is not Christianity which has sustained social evil. All through our history, colonial and national, the hope and ambition of every young man and woman have been for a home of their own, into which one husband and one wife shall enter, "and they twain shall be one flesh." One of the sad features of city life to-day is the crowding into apartments, where the janitor is master of the house and the independence of the home life is only partially secured.

The barracks around our great manufacturing establishments are freighted with equally sad significance. While admitting this temporary departure we rejoice that this has been pre-eminently a land of homes, whether in the city, or village, or country. And the power which has ever stood in the land for the purity of home life has been a crown of glory to the republic.

Christianity has stood for business honesty and integrity. Its proclamation has been the golden rule. "Do unto others as you would have them do unto you" is a summons to honesty and fair dealing in all business as well as other relations in life. The Master never suggested that ability to keep outside the penitentiary was a sufficient test of honesty.

CIVIL LIBERTY

Christianity has stood for liberty and the rights of man. In the great revolutionary struggle, the trusted counselors of the people were the preachers. While they may not be known in history as the leaders, while they were not the lawyers to draft the statutes and the constitution nor the military heroes to command the armies, yet the local centers of influence were the Christian churches, and the Christian preachers were the men who kept the mass of the people loyal to the leadership of Washington and his associates.

EDUCATION

Christianity has stood for education. I have already called your attention to this matter in proof of the Christian character of the nation. It may be added that outside of the institutions with direct State support nearly every academy, college and university was founded by and is under the control of some one of the several Christian denominations. Indeed, a frequent criticism of many is that they are too much under such control. Certain is it that they would never have come into being but for the denominations back of them. Up to a recent date the rule was that the presidents and an exceedingly large majority of the faculty of all these institutions be ministers. It was a national surprise when first a layman was elected a college president.

In the common schools the Bible has been as much a textbook as the New England Primer. It is only within very late years that any objection has been raised to its daily use, and that objection was sprung as much from differences between the Catholic and Protestant denominations concerning the version to be used as from opposition to the book itself.

CHARITY

Christianity has stood for the great charities and benevolences of the land. What single organization has done more for the orphan than the Catholic Church? What one, through hospital and asylum, more for the sick and afflicted? If you were to select a single face and form as the typical expression of the great thought of charity and kindness, whose would you select other than the face and form of a Sister of Charity?

"The Little Sister of the Poor"

Amid the city's dust and din
Your patient feet have trod;
Wherever sorrow is or sin
You do the work of God.

You seem in many a shadowed place
A glory from above,
The peace of heaven is in your face,
And in your heart is love.

Your brow is lined with others' cares,
And aches for others' needs;
You bless the dying with your prayers,
The living with your deeds.

You sow the wayside hope that lives
Where else were only death;
Your love is like the rain that gives
Heaven's secret to the earth.

The pitying thoughts that fill your eyes,
And rob your years of rest,

That lead you still where misery sighs
And life is all unblest,

Are as the tears that angels shed
O'er darkened lives forlorn—
Stars in the gloom till night has fled,
And dew on earth at morn.

In times when epidemics rage, when death seems to haunt every city home, who are the devoted ones to risk their lives in caring for the sick and paying the last offices to the dead? Surely as the vision of this rises in your mind you see the presence and form of those whose faith is in the Man of Galilee.

HARMONY AND ORDER

Christianity has stood for peace. I need not content myself by referring to that Christian denomination, one of whose distinguishing tenets is unqualified opposition to all wars. I can with safety point to the great body of those who in days gone by have been the champions of the cause of peace; to the memorials which have been presented to the two Houses of Congress in favor of arbitration; to those who are at the head of the various peace societies, and who are always found upon the platforms at their gatherings, and whose voices are most constant and potent in its behalf. Indeed, strike from the history of this country all that the Christian Church has done in the interest and to further the cause of peace and there is not as much life left as was found in the barren fig tree.

Christianity has stood for temperance. Not that it has stood alone, but it has been a leader. The foremost advocates of the cause have been pronounced Christians. Frances Willard was president of the Woman's Christian Temperance Union, not of the Woman's Mohammedan Temperance Union, and the White Ribboners are not disciples of Confucius or Buddha. The churches have been the places of the great gatherings of the friends of temperance. Indeed, when you survey the efforts made to further that cause you will find that running through them all Christianity has been distinctively present.

In short, Christianity has sought to write into the history of this nation the glowing words of the apostle: "Love, joy, peace, long-suffering, gentleness, goodness, faith, meekness, temperance; against such there is no law."

Christianity has stood for all these things because they represent its thought and purpose. So he who studies the history of the country, finding this to be the lesson of its influence upon our history, can but be led to the conclusion not merely that it has been a potent factor in the life of the nation, but also that it has been a healthful and helpful factor. When one who loves his country realizes this fact, does there not open before him a clear vision of his duty to further its influence? If in the past it has done so much and so well for the country is there any reason to doubt that strengthened and extended it will continue the same healthful and helpful influence?

It has been often said that Christian nations are the civilized nations, and as often that the most thoroughly Christian are the most highly civilized. Is this a mere coincidence? Study well the history of Christianity in its relation to the nation and it will be found that it is something more than a mere coincidence, that there is between the two the relation of cause and effect, and that the more thoroughly the principles of Christianity reach into and influence the life of the nation the more certainly will that nation advance in civilization. At least it is the duty of every patriot, finding that it has been such a factor in our life, to inquire whether it does stand to its civilization in the relation of cause and effect, and it would be in the highest degree unphilosophical to assume that there has been only a coincidence, and therefore that its presence in the nation is a matter of indifference.

If found that Christianity has been both a potent and helpful factor in the development of our civilization, then it is a patriot's duty to uphold it and extend its influence. This is in line with the general obligation which rests upon all to help everything which tends to the bettering of the life of the republic. Who does not recognize that obligation in other directions?

THE DUTY OF THE CITIZEN TO PRESERVE AMERICA

Today a prevalent belief is that in order to maintain our position in the world, a position which has rapidly changed from one of isolation to that of intimate relation with all nations, we ought to pay larger attention to our navy. If that belief is well founded, if it be true that a larger and more efficient navy is essential to the maintenance of our position in the world, then who will question the duty of every citizen? May we antagonize that which the nation's interests demand? Shall we through selfishness or indifference permit that which means the well-being and glory of the nation to become weak or to fail altogether? Who hesitates about the answer to such a question? So with our commerce. Is it not a praiseworthy effort on the part of each and all to enlarge that commerce and thus to add to the prosperity which attends a successful world commerce?

Or to come closer to those things which touch the social and moral well-being of the nation, who doubts a patriot's duty to further the cause of education? Who questions that the best interests of the republic are prompted by extending education to all? And can anyone, doing justice to himself, and without violating his duty to the republic, plead that he is wholly indifferent to the matter?

Take another illustration—civil service reform. I shall not enter into any argument in its favor. I assume that the principle of it commends itself to the thoughtful as something which, wisely administered, will eliminate much of the pitiful scramble for office and secure a better administration of public affairs. Upon that assumption, who does not feel that he has a duty in so far as in him lies to further the movement in its favor? It may be that it has not yet accomplished that which its friends believe it possible of accomplishing; that much is to be done before it is placed upon a permanent and efficient basis. And yet if it be something which in its development will overflow to the national well-being is there not a duty resting upon all to strengthen and perfect it?

Now these are mere illustrations of the duty which, as patriotic citizens, we all feel in reference to those measures which tend to promote the well-being of the republic. Upon what grounds may we recognize our obligations in these directions and decline to do anything to extend and make more efficient the principles of Christianity? I am not now presenting this as a question affecting the life hereafter. I am putting it before you simply as a citizen's duty, as a matter affecting only the well-being and glory of the republic.

You may concede that, as illustrated by the lives of its professed followers, Christianity comes far short of what you think it ought to be, and yet if you believe that its spirit and principles are freighted with blessing to the individual as well as to the nation, is it not an obvious duty to seek to purify it in the individual and strengthen it in the nation? The selfish spirit is not a commendable element in the life of a true citizen. It is as old as Scripture that no man liveth unto himself alone, and in the marvelously and increasingly intimate relations of individuals one to the other and the growing power of the citizen over the life of the nation, the unselfish patriot must always consider not simply his own interests, his own comfort and convenience, but those things which make for the well-being of all.

The significance of this duty has another aspect. The idea that "No man liveth unto himself alone" may be broadened into "No nation liveth unto itself alone." Neighbor is no longer confined to the vocabulary of the individual. It is a national word. Modern inventions have annihilated distance. Commercial relations have broken down barriers of race and religion, and the family of nations is a recognized fact.

This republic has joined in the movement of the age. She no longer lives an isolated life separated by the oceans from the great powers of the world. She sits in the councils of the nations and we rejoice to speak of her and hear her spoken of as a world power. Indeed, some begin to think ambitiously of this republic as a sort of international policeman, with the right to exercise all the functions of a policeman in preserving order and keeping peace. The Monroe Doctrine is to be extended. No longer simply a prohibition upon further European colonies, but a declaration that if any European power claims anything from any nation on this hemisphere it must appeal to the United States and not attempt to assert by force its claims. We propose to administer the estate of San Domingo, even before its death. We intend to preserve the integrity of China. We intimated to Russia that the Jews must no longer be persecuted. We are disposed to say to Turkey that Armenian life and property must be safe, and we hear, as the Apostle of old, the cry, "Come over into Macedonia and help us."

I do not stop to discuss whether we are not overdoing in this direction; whether it is wise wholly to forget Washington's farewell advice to avoid entangling alliances with other nations. Neither shall I attempt to criticize the recently announced maxim of national duty, "speak softly, but carry a big stick." But of one thing I am sure: In no other way can this republic become a world power in the noblest sense of the word than by putting into her life and the lives of her citizens the spirit and principles of the great founder of Christianity.

We have faith in the future of the United States. We believe she will advance in many directions. She may increase her territory, add to her population, her commerce may grow larger, her accumulations in wealth surpass the wildest dreams of the Pilgrim Fathers, her inventive skill subject all the forces of nature to do her bidding and surround every home with comforts and luxuries unknown even to the present day. Besides her statues and paintings, the chiseled beauties of Phidias and the pictured splendors of Raphael may seem the works of tyros, her literature may dwarf all the achievements of the writers and thinkers of ages past, and thus she may tower in greatness in the sight of the world. But grander far, and far more potential over the nations will America be, when the Beatitudes become the magna charta of her life and her citizens live in full obedience to the Golden Rule. Then, and not until then, will all nations and their peoples join rejoicingly with our citizens in this triumphal song to the great republic:

> *Thou, too, sail on, oh Ship of State!*
> *Sail on, oh, Union, strong and great!*
> *Humanity with all its fears,*
> *With all the hopes of future years,*
> *Is hanging breathless on thy fate!*
> *We know what Master laid thy keel,*
> *What workmen wrought thy ribs of steel,*
> *Who made each mast, and sail, and rope,*
> *What anvils rang, what hammers beat.*

In what a forge and what a heat
Were shaped the anchors of thy hope!
Fear trot each sudden sound and shock,
'Tis of the wave and not the rock;
'Tis but the flapping of the sail,
And not a rent made by the gale!
In spite of rock and tempest's roar,
In spite of false lights on the shore,
Sail on, nor fear to breast the sea!
Our hearts, our hopes, are all with thee,
Our hearts, our hopes, our prayers, our tears,
Our faith triumphant o'er our fears,
Are all with thee—are all with thee!

LECTURE III

The Promise and Possibilities of the Future

"...there is no incompatibility between Christianity and patriotism."

LECTURE III

The Promise and Possibilities of the Future

AND NOW, WHAT OF THE FUTURE? IF CHRISTIANITY HAS BEEN so largely identified with the life of this nation and identified in a helpful and blessed way, what promise and possibilities does it bring of the future? Of course, whatever tends to the better life of the individual helps to promote the welfare of the nation. Anything that conduces to personal purity, morality, and integrity increases the same characteristics in the community. It needs no declaration of Scripture to convince that "righteousness exalteth a nation; but sin is a reproach to any people."

In so far, therefore, as the principles and precepts of Christianity develop righteousness in the individual, to the same extent will a similar result be found in the life of the nation. This subject in its general features opens the door to extended discussion and is susceptible of many illustrations. The contrast between the standard of life in a heathen and that in a Christian nation shows the range of examination into which we may enter.

AMERICA THE MELTING POT

Out of the wide field of illustration, let me call your attention to one or two matters in which the Christian character of this republic shines out with richest promise. One arises from the fact that this nation is composed of people of various races and not wholly or even substantially of one. We all have read the story of the dispersion at Babel. That story may not be the narration of an actual experience, yet it is a correct foreshadowing of the world's history. In whatsoever way it commenced, through all the ages the inhabitants of the globe have been gathered in separate localities, each race or tribe occupying its own locality. The history of the world is one long story of strife between nation and nation, tribe and tribe, race and race. And everywhere today, except here, we find within the territory of a nation one race alone, or so nearly alone, that it is supremely dominant. You go to Germany and the Germans are there, forming the substantial controlling part of the population. There may be a few foreigners engaged in business or travel, some may even make it their home, but it is a German nation pure and simple, and the other races have no place in its life. In France, Russia, Turkey, it is the same. But in this republic it is different, and no race monopolizes American life. The dispersion at Babel has ended on the banks of the Mississippi. And the races that once separated and have continued separate and antagonistic for untold centuries are mingling here in a common life.

While all doubtless have in a general way some notion of the many foreigners in our midst, few realize the extent to which this nation is made up of different races. Let me give a few figures taken from the census of 1900. The total population was 76,000,000, of which 67,000,000 were white and 9,000,000 colored. That is one race, 9,000,000, out of the 76,000,000. Of the white population there were of native parentage 41,000,000, of foreign, 26,000,000. Of the latter, 10,000,000 were also of foreign birth; and when you speak of foreign parentage you must remember that almost all of us, going back two or three generations, will find foreign ancestors. Of the 26,000,000 of foreign parentage there were (counting by hundreds of thousands) from Austria, 400,000; Bohemia, 400,000; Canada, 2,100,000; Denmark, 300,000; England, 2,100,000; France, 300,000; Italy, 700,000; Germany, 7,800,000; Hungary, 200,000; Ireland, 5,000,000; Norway, 800,000; Poland, 700,000; Russia, 700,000; Scotland, 600,000; Sweden, 1,100,000; Switzerland, 300,000; Wales, 200,000; other nations, 1,100,000, and of mixed parentage 1,300,000.

This multitude is here, not as travelers, not with a view of temporary sojourn, but to make this their home. They are invited under our law to become citizens, sharing with us the duties and responsibilities of citizenship, so that we have gathered as members of our nation hundreds of thousands from almost every race on the face of the globe. They come, bringing with them that antagonism of race which has continued for centuries. The old quarrels are not forgotten. They bring with them differences in habits and thoughts, in political hopes and convictions, differences of religious faith, and in many instances a lack of any faith. They come and are merged into the life of this nation, and are, as you and I, to make its destiny. They form part of the forces which are to shape the future of this country.

Some think, or say they think, that there is no such thing as an overruling Providence, that we are mere atoms of matter tossed to and fro on the face of the earth, and that here is the beginning and the end. They do not take into thought the great life of the ages, or measure its movements from its first feeble steps; and yet they sometimes feel compelled to admit that it seems as though there were something more than mere blind chance. I remember that Speaker Reed once said in a public address (I am not quoting his exact words) that while he himself was not much of a believer in special providences, it did seem as though these things—referring to some of the great events of history—were brought about by an intelligent and infinite Being. You may fancy that the mingling of all these races in this country is a mere accident; that it simply happened so. And yet if you will reflect a little you will be led to the conclusion that, as Tennyson writes: "Through the ages one increasing purpose runs."

Four centuries ago the nations in the then known world were living their isolated and separate lives. Racial antagonism was persistent. There was little intercourse between them. Education was practically unknown. There were a few learned men here and there. The common people were crushed to earth. Religion, the religion of Christ, was largely buried beneath a mass of superstitions. The Bible was a chained book. The world was creeping on through the darkness of the Middle Ages, and the morning seemed away off in the distance.

Then Gutenberg invented printing. Luther said the Bible must be an open book. The masses began to read and dream of liberty. Columbus declared that there was a land away to the west, he journeyed in little caravels across the ocean, and America was discovered. To the temperate part of this western continent came the Huguenot from France, the Pilgrim from England, the persecuted from different lands, and settled along the Atlantic shore. Religion was a potent factor in the settlement of these colonies.

Now, is it not strange that by mere chance, printing, a free Bible, an unoccupied country, and an absorbing desire for greater liberty should come about the same time, and that as the outcome of this coincidence there should settle upon the virgin soil of this new continent colonies escaping from persecution and bringing here education, liberty, and religion? And then is it not singular that to this new continent there should come through the years that followed, from every race on the face of the globe, a multitude seeking a new home, settling beneath the Stars and Stripes, feeling that in some way or other this was the place where the great destinies of the future were to be wrought out? Is this all accidental? Does it not suggest that in the councils of eternity, long before man began to be, it was planned that here in this republic should be worked out the unity of the race—a unity made possible by the influences of education and the power of Christianity? Certainly, to me it is a supreme conviction, growing stronger and stronger as the years go by, that this is one purpose of Providence in the life of this republic, and that to this end we are to take from every race its strongest and best elements and characteristics, and mold and fuse them into one homogeneous American life.

THE CHARACTER OF COMMUNITY

Some of you know something about composite photography, and how face after face is thrown upon the same plate until a picture is produced which is a representation of thirty or forty faces, one upon another. As you look at this composite picture you see that the marked and strong characteristics of each face are visible, while the weak ones are lost. America is the great national photographer. She takes from every race its best elements and is to mold them into one American character.

What does all this mean? If there be a purpose running through the life of the world, is it not plain that one thought in the divine plan was that in this republic should be unfolded and developed in the presence of the world the Christian doctrine of the fatherhood of God and the brotherhood of man? To the full realization of this, something more is necessary than a mere uniting in the active duties of our daily life; something more than interracial marriages bringing the races into one common stock; something more than a mingling in toil, whether on the farm, in the shop, the factory or the office, the working together in the same political parties, or the prosecution of the same lines of study and identification in all material interests. Beyond all this must be developed the essentials of a pure family life, a community of thought and purpose in those higher things which make for the betterment of all.

It is not that here one race shall be enabled to rise to the fullest development of its capacity, while all other races are ministering to that uplifting, but rather that each and every one of every race should be given the amplest opportunity for his own elevation. No perfect family exists where one is bound down with the lower duties in order that another shall rise. It exists only when each is given the fullest possible scope for his own uprising. There will always be diversity of work, but the open door must be before every one.

For the realization of this, can anything be more potent than the golden rule, the presence of the spirit of Christianity? Under its power each will be faithful in the work he does, while evermore to him is outstretched the helping hand of all. And so it will be that all races mingling in the common American life will give to it of their best, and here, first of all, will be realized the fulfillment of the final prayer of the Master in the Upper Chamber, "That they all may be one; as Thou, Father, art in me, and I in Thee." Surely this republic may glory in the opportunity through its Christian life and power of winning for herself the great glory of such achievement.

THE WEALTH OF THE NATIONS

Another door of promise is open in the opportunity before America of realizing within her borders the highest standard of life. One of the pressing dangers facing all civilized nations is the enervating influence of wealth and great material development. That was the one thing which sapped the life of the great nations of antiquity and buried them in the tombs of their own vices. In each there was a wonderful accumulation of wealth, marvelous manifestations of material splendor, but the moral character of their citizens was undermined thereby and they declined and fell. The hanging gardens of Babylon, the pyramids of Egypt, the sculptured beauty which lined the streets of Athens, and all that luxurious display which attended the centering in Rome of the products of the civilizations of the earth in their day provoked the admiration and were the boast of their citizens. They passed through the same round of experience. Wealth brought luxury, luxury brought vice, and vice was followed by ruin and decay. And now we dig through the accumulating dust of centuries to find even the ruins of their vanished splendor.

Today we are in the presence of a similar marvelous material development. It is one of the phenomena which attracts everybody's attention. You hear on all sides descriptions of the wonderful things which the scientific mind and the ingenious skill of the country is accomplishing. The skyscrapers, the tunnels, the railroads, the mighty steamships, the telegraph, the cable, the telephone, all these things, with their accompanying conveniences and luxuries, are before us. I am not here to say anything against the magnificence of this material development, but, remember, it is only a means to an end. We do not live to make bricks and mortar, nor to build skyscrapers. You go on the banks of the Nile, and there, rivalling all that we have built, stand those gloomy, lofty pyramids, as they have stood for century after century, looking out over the silent sands, speaking no word to humanity of cheer and encouragement, telling no tale of something done for the betterment of the race, and in their cold, sad solitude witnesses only to unrequited toil in behalf of men whose names have almost vanished from history.

Macaulay, in one of his beautiful essays, suggests that possibly the time may come when some South Sea Islander will stand on the broken arches of London Bridge, looking upon the deserted ruins of that city and wondering at the civilization that in it once prevailed. That which alone will save this country from the destiny which has attended those nations which have vanished into oblivion, that which will make our marvelous material development something for the glory of humanity and the upbuilding and permanence of this republic, is the putting into the life of the nation the conviction that the purpose and end of all is the building up of a better manhood and womanhood.

How is this to be accomplished? Not certainly by giving up all our thought to material development. "As a man thinketh, so is he." And if the nation puts all its energies and thought into simply the work of extending its commerce, improving its highways, building up great cities and adding to its manufactures, it may expect the fate which attended those departed nations.

Neither is it accomplished by any inculcation of the merely utilitarian philosophy of a selfish morality. Honesty undoubtedly is the best policy. It is a maxim, good in itself, but if the only thought is of the pecuniary results of such a policy it will fail. He who is honest in his dealings simply because of the social prestige and position it secures will never develop his higher nature, but will always live along the lower lines.

You must fill the soul with the impulses of the higher spirit of righteousness, the spirit that makes justice and uprightness things to be sought after because of their own blessed influences upon the individual—that spirit which is measured not by its capacity for coinage into dollars, but by its power upon the life. The better life rests less on the prohibitions of the Ten Commandments and more on the parable of the Good Samaritan and the Golden Rule. The rich man who came to the Master declared in reference to the Commandments, "All these have I kept from my youth up," but his weakness was pierced by the searching reply, "One thing thou yet lackest; go, sell whatsoever thou hast and follow me." In other words, Christianity, entering into the life of the individual, and thus into the life of the nation, is the only sure antidote for the poisonous touch of mere material prosperity. Do you ever doubt the outcome, or dread to think of the possible future of the republic? Remember that:

> *Behind the dim unknown,*
> *Standeth God within the shadow, keeping*
> *watch above His own.*

WHEN WAR SHALL CEASE

Another illustration is in its influence for peace in the world. Christianity is called the gospel of peace. Among the names which in prophecy were ascribed to its founder is that of "Prince of Peace." At the time of His birth it is said that the doors of the Temple of Janus in Rome were closed by reason of the fact that peace for the time being prevailed in all the nations. Among the last words to His disciples in the upper chamber were, "Peace I leave with you." The dream of the warring world has ever been of the coming of a time when peace should prevail. War, however just, however righteous, is attended with unspeakable horrors. All accept General Sherman's characterization that "war is hell."

It is to the glory of this nation that it has already done so much in the interests of peace and to minimize the horrors of war. In Jay's Treaty with Great Britain, in 1794, there were stipulations against the confiscation of debts due from the individuals of the one nation to individuals of the other, and for the peaceful residence of citizens of either nation in the territory of the other during the continuance of the war. At the time of the French Revolution our government issued stringent orders in respect to the preservation of neutrality—so stringent as to call from Mr. Hall, the recent leading English writer on international law, the declaration that "the policy of the United States in 1793 constitutes an epoch in the development of the usages of neutrality." During the administration of Mr. Monroe our government proposed to France, England, and Russia, that in times of war merchant vessels and their cargoes belonging to subjects of belligerent powers should be exempt from capture. While we did not assent in 1856 to the Declaration of Paris, by which privateering was abolished, we offered to agree to it if the nations would consent that private property on the seas should be free from capture. Since then we have agreed to the abolition of privateering.

The proclamations of our Presidents at the commencements of recent wars and the decisions of our Supreme Court have been along the line of ameliorating the hardships of war. We stood with Great Britain at The Hague Conference as the most earnest advocates of the establishment of an international arbitration tribunal, and in the Orient, China, and Japan each recognize this government as of all, the most free from selfish motives in its treatment of them and action for them. The integrity of China depends on this republic, and the territorial limits of the present war have been narrowed at our instance. Our international relations have been lifted from the lower to a higher plane. Diplomatic language is no longer a means of concealing, but of expressing thought and

58

purpose. Neither Machiavelli nor Tallyrand is the type of American diplomacy.

Does the day of peace seem a long way off? Think of the ages upon ages during which, even within the limits of a nation with its compact and unifying forces, has been evolving the supremacy of right over might and the settlement of disputes by judicial action rather than physical force. We have no reason to expect a speedy coming of the day when the judicial function will settle all disputes between nations. A nation may be born in a day, but the great truths which make for the glory and uplift of the race only through long ages permeate and control humanity. We must have the divine patience and understand the divine mathematics of a thousand years as one day.

There will yet be wars and rumors of wars. Our own loved land will not be exempt. The cry for a larger navy will long be a party slogan. The air will be resonant with the blare of bugles. The tramp, tramp, of armed battalions will be along our streets. Statues of our great commanders will be seen in all our parks and buildings, and present history will be filled with the story of military and naval achievements. But the leaven of the immortal truth that right rather than might attests the ideal life is already working in the mass of humanity, and slowly it will leaven the whole lump. I am not here to make light of the patriotic devotion of our military and naval heroes. I would not take one jot or tittle from all the glory which attends our army and navy and crowns with laurel its heroes. But at the same time I want to affirm my faith that the laurels of peace are more enduring than those of war.

Time, which is the Almighty's great right hand of recompense, will brighten the one while it dims the other. John Marshall will be remembered when Winfield Scott is forgotten. In the far off future the names of our greatest commanders will fill a lessening space in the horizon of history, while with ever brightening splendor will shine the name of America's peace-loving and golden-rule diplomat, Secretary John Hay. The measure of fame will be meted out by Him who has declared that He will lay judgment to the line and righteousness to the plummet. Is not it a great thing to be a leader among the nations in the effort to bring on that day when the sword shall be beaten into the ploughshare and the spear into the pruning hook, and when war shall cease? And the more thoroughly this republic is filled with the spirit of the gospel, the more universal the rule of Christianity in the hearts of our people, the more certainly will she ever be the welcome leader in movements for peace among the nations.

Nineteen centuries ago there broke upon the startled ears of Judea's shepherds watching their flocks beside the village of Bethlehem, the only angel's song ever heard by the children of earth:

> *It came upon the midnight clear,*
> *That glorious song of old,*
> *From angels bending near the earth*
> *To touch their harps of gold:*
> *"Peace on the earth, good-will to men*
> *From Heaven's all gracious king."*

The air above Judea's plains no longer pulsates with the waves of this celestial song. For sad and weary centuries the march of humanity upwards has been through strife and blood. But a growing echo of the heavenly music is filling the hearts of men and the time will come, the blessed time will come

> *When the whole world gives back the song*
> *Which now the angels sing.*

THE TRANSFORMING LIFE OF JESUS

One thing more. Whatever difference of opinion there may be as to the divinity of the Man of Galilee, His position as a man is confessedly supreme. Renan, the brilliant French writer, closed his life of Christ with these words:

Whatever the unexpected phenomena of the future, Jesus will never be surpassed. His worship will constantly renew its youth, the legend of His life will bring ceaseless tears, His sufferings will soften the best hearts; all the ages will proclaim that, amongst the sons of men, none has been born who is greater than Jesus.

By common consent He stands the most potent individual force for the highest things of life. How strange it is that a Galilean youth, away from the centers of civilization, untaught in the schools, living a humble life among country people, familiar with poverty and having no place whereon to lay His head, dying at the age of thirty-three, after only three years of public presentation of Himself, at the time making so little impression on the life of the world that only a single word or two respecting Him is found in the records of Rome, the great center of civilization—should now, after the lapse of nineteen centuries, be revered as Divine by millions upon millions, be universally acknowledged as the most uplifting power known to humanity and whose power is ever widening until it touches all quarters of the globe.

Faith in Him goes hand in hand with the highest civilization, and all realize that the more His spirit enters into one's life the better that life becomes. In the light of this admitted fact, can any one look thoughtfully upon the future of this nation without believing that if His spirit shall become more and more potent, not merely the individual citizens, but the nation as a whole will rise in all the elements of moral grandeur and power?

THE FUTURE OF AMERICA

With patriotic and prophetic vision we see our beloved country advancing, not alone along the lines of material prosperity and accumulating wealth, but also along the better lines of increasing intelligence and a loftier sense of duty. We see her quickened by the ennobling power of the golden rule, and the spirit of the Good Samaritan, bidding all her citizens to seek first the kingdom of God and its righteousness; introducing into the vocabulary of international law the blessed word neighbor, and leading humanity along the kindly ways of peace and mutual helpfulness until "out of every kindred, and tongue, and people, and nation" shall rise a glad psalm of thanksgiving and joy that in the good Providence of the Almighty there has been planted upon these western shores the living and growing tree of liberty, education and Christian principles.

Young gentlemen, to you, as to comparatively few in the long lapse of centuries, comes the magnificent opportunity. Before you is the open door to great achievement and great usefulness. With rich endowment of youth, health, friends, and education you stand in the morning hours of that which is to be a century of unsurpassed significance. We look back on the last fifty years as years of wonderful scientific development and marvelous inventions, yet Lord Kelvin, perhaps the greatest scientist of today, said in substance, not long since, that, wonderful as have been the accomplishments in these respects during those years, we are trembling on the verge of inventions and discoveries as far surpassing them as they do any that have gone before. That declaration coming from such a mind was and is prophetic. Since then wireless telegraphy has come, and who shall guess the next marvel?

The spirit of liberty is shaking thrones and dynasties the world over, and making government of the people, by the people, and for the people, a nearer fact. Even that great embodiment of despotism among civilized nations, Russia, is now rocking from one end to the other through its dynamic explosions. Education is sweeping through the world and the common school is lifting the masses up to a higher level and a stronger citizenship. Engineering skill seems to know no limits. Time and space are abolished. Steam is slow and giving place to electricity. Gigantic combinations of capital grapple without hesitation gigantic schemes of improvement. Overflowing streams of commerce circle the world. The human brain is under constant strain. Life has become strenuous. Every one is throwing into the great cauldron of public opinion some scheme or plan or idea, practical or visionary, sensible or foolish, until it seems as though beside that cauldron were ever present the witches of Macbeth chanting:

> *Double, double, toil and trouble;*
> *Fire burn, and cauldron bubble.*

Out of this tremendous activity, these gigantic combinations, will come achievements marvelous beyond even the flights of fancy. Into this century with all its possibilities you enter as young men. You have the grasp of a lifetime upon them. Your presence in this institution is to fit yourselves to take part in those achievements. I know not what may be your respective places in life. The avenues of labor and usefulness are many and pointing in diverse directions. Business, science, art, medicine, law, theology, all are before you. In no country on the face of the globe is there an equal opportunity for the individual brain and the personal force. There is that freedom which gives ample scope for individual activities. All that you do and achieve will enter into and become part of the national glory or the national shame. You can make your names honored ones in the history of the republic, or by-words and a reproach. You may repeat the story of Alexander Hamilton or that of Aaron Burr. I cannot doubt your choice and purpose. No man covets infamy, and the young, thank God, have lofty ideals.

> *Fear not to build thine eyrie in the heights*
> *Where golden splendors play;*
> *And trust thyself unto thine inmost soul,*
> *In simple faith alway;*
> *For God will make divinely real*
> *The highest forms of thine ideal.*

How can those ideals be best incorporated into your lives and thus into the life of the nation? You know what a Christian home is, even if not brought up in one. Whether a humble one with scanty furnishings, or a more pretentious one with costlier adornments, in each you found truthfulness, purity; the spirit of peace was upon it; industry dwelt there, self-respect in the individual and mutual respect in all. Will you add one more to the many of those homes in the land? You can bring to it strength and ability to work. You can bring cultivated intelligence and the delights of literature and science. You may introduce into it the sweet and refining touch of music and the other arts. You may place on the other side of the table the angel of the household, whose gentleness and grace add so much to the sweetness of home life.

Crown all these with the inspirations which come from Christianity, place the Bible on your table and enshrine the Master in your heart and you may be sure you are building up a home which will be not merely peace and blessing to you, but also for the strength and glory of the republic. And when the evening of life comes nigh and you see such homes multiply in the land, this nation becomes more thoroughly filled with the spirit and principles of Christianity, more justly and universally entitled to the appellation of a Christian nation, you will sing with Julia Ward Howe: "Mine eyes have seen the glory of the coming of the Lord."

THE HOLY TRINITY CASE

A Legacy of Liberty

BY HERBERT W. TITUS, J.D.

The U.S. Supreme Court

THE HOLY TRINITY CASE

A Legacy of Liberty

BY HERBERT W. TITUS, J.D.

STATING THE CASE

The Supreme Court case *The Church of the Holy Trinity v. United States* possesses none of the attributes that one would expect of a cause celebre. It began innocently as a misdemeanor prosecution for violation of an immigration statute. The Church of the Holy Trinity, an incorporated religious society, had contracted an Englishman by the name of E. Walpole Warren to come to New York and become the church's rector and pastor. The United States government responded by charging the church with violation of a law that forbade "any person, company, partnership of corporation" from making any contract "for labor or service of any kind" that would "in any way assist or encourage the importation or migration of any alien...or foreigner...into the United States...."[1]

At trial, the church did not defend itself by raising a First Amendment claim of freedom of religion. Nor did it interpose any other constitu-

---

Herbert W. Titus received a bachelor of science degree in political science from the University of Oregon and a doctorate of jurisprudence from Harvard University Law School. Dr. Titus has worked as a trial attorney with the U.S. Department of Justice and as a professor of law at various state universities and at Oral Roberts University. He also served eleven years at Regent University, first as the founding Dean of the School of Public Policy, then as Vice-President for Academic Affairs, and finally as the founding Dean of the School of Law. Presently, Dr. Titus practices law in Virginia Beach, Virginia, specializing in constitutional litigation and strategy. He is the author of numerous articles and monographs and a book entitled *God, Man and Law: The Biblical Principles*. Dr. Titus also publishes *The Forecast*, a monthly journal on law and public policy.

tional objection. Instead, the church's sole defense was that the statute should not be interpreted to prohibit a contract between a church and a foreign pastor.

The Church of the Holy Trinity based its argument on the part of the statute which provided a list of exceptions, but which did not include the employment of pastors. Therefore, the defense was rejected, and the church was found guilty as charged. The church lost its first appeal before the case finally reached the United States Supreme Court.

THE LETTER VERSUS THE INTENT OF THE LAW

At the outset of his opinion, Justice David Brewer, writing for a unanimous Court, conceded that "the letter of" the law supported the previous rulings that the church's contract with Mr. Walpole was illegal. He and his colleagues, however, refused to be bound by literal reading of the statute, claiming that such a meaning would lead to a manifestly "absurd" result.

At first, Justice Brewer labored mightily to show that unless the Court narrowed the scope of the statute's rather broad and sweeping language, it would thwart its real purpose.[2] What prompted Congress to pass the law, Justice Brewer contended, was the practice of "large capitalists in this country" who made contracts with "an ignorant and servile class of foreign laborers...at a low rate of wages," and, thereby, broke down "the labor market" and "reduce[d] other laborers engaged in like occupations to the level of the assisted immigrant."[3]

Turning to the Congressional Record, Justice Brewer concluded that Congress was only addressing the problem raised by contracts with unskilled laborers from foreign countries, not the employment of alien professionals. Therefore, he decided that the reach of the statute should be confined to contracts for "manual labor," not for professional services, like the services of a pastor.

AMERICA: A CHRISTIAN NATION

Had Justice Brewer rested his case on this reasoning alone, the Court could not have justified its ruling. The plain language of the statute clearly prohibited contracts for "service of any kind" as well as for "labor of any kind." Whatever the events prompting the statute's enactment, and whatever the testimony offered in support, the language was both comprehensive and all-encompassing, admitting only a few explicit exceptions, none of which allowed the employment of a foreign pastor.

Mindful that the Court could be accused of having simply rewritten the statute, Justice Brewer launched what he believed to be the decisive reason why the statute could not be construed to prohibit a contract between a church and a pastor. To do so, he asserted, would be to place the federal government "against religion." This, he wrote, should never be "imputed to any legislation, State or Nation, because this is a religious people."[4]

To support this rule of statutory construction, Justice Brewer surveyed the history of the nation from the time of Columbus's discovery to the date of the opinion, concluding that America was, and is, "a Christian nation." Hence, he decided no statute should be construed to interfere with the work of the Church, unless the language explicitly required it.

In his remarkable summary of the role of religion in the founding of America and its continued prosperity as a nation, Justice Brewer made two salient points, equally relevant to the statutory issue before the Court.

First, he noted that America's founders had come to the Americas pursuant to the Great Commission, that is, to advance the Christian faith.[5] That purpose, he claimed, had never changed, from the earliest colonizations to 1892, nearly three hundred years later:

> [C]hurches and church organizations...abound in every city town, and hamlet;...[a] multitude of charitable organizations exist...everywhere under Christian auspices;...gigantic missionary associations, with general support,...aim...to establish Christian missions in every quarter of the globe.[6]

If the statute before the Court were to be construed to prohibit a church's choice of pastoral leadership, it would hinder the work of the church, an absurd result in a nation dedicated to the advancement of the Christian faith.

Secondly, Justice Brewer observed, the American people had established civil orders, according to the laws of God. These godly orders reinforced the nation's founding purpose, to advance the Christian faith.[7] And they did so in two distinct ways.

They embraced Christian principles as the foundation for all laws of civil obligation. "[T]he Christian religion," Justice Brewer reminded his readers, is, and always has been, a "part of the common law."[8] Thus, he noted, the nation as a whole was required to adhere to those moral standards that are designed to maintain order in the community, such as laws ordaining one day of rest during the week.[9]

At the same time, Brewer remembered that it was Christianity that gave rise to the laws of civil liberty. The Christian legal heritage of the American republic was that of "liberty of conscience to all men." This regime of freedom, he wrote, limited the power of the nation and the states to those matters within its jurisdiction. Included within this area of liberty was the right to promote the Christian religion, and even to promote other faiths, without interference from the civil government.[10]

MATTERS OF CHURCH AND STATE

Given this consistent and corporate Christian heritage of law and liberty, Justice Brewer asked this question:

[S]hall it be believed that a Congress of the United States intended to make it a misdemeanor for a church of this country to contract for the services of a Christian minister residing in another nation?[11]

He answered this question with a simple appeal to America's great legacy of liberty. Surely, no one could possibly claim that Congress would pass a law intentionally designed to limit the right of a church or synagogue or other religious organization to contract with the spiritual leader of its choice. Such matters are presumed to be totally outside the civil realm.[12] Hence, to read a statute as if it prohibited such a contract without explicit language manifesting that intent would be absurd.

Thus, Justice Brewer concluded that the Court would not construe the language of the statute to intrude upon the work of the church, thereby hindering the furtherance of the Gospel and interfering with the free exercise of religion. Had Justice Brewer not adhered to America's Christian heritage of law and liberty, he could not have justified the conclusion that he did.

While the issue before in the *Holy Trinity* case was simply a matter of statutory construction, the Court's rule favoring liberty over government control was made possible by America's history as a Christian nation. That legacy, contrary to popular opinion one hundred years later, is, above all, a legacy of liberty, denying to Caesar those matters that belong exclusively to God.

NOTES

1. *The Church of the Holy Trinity v. United States* (1892), 143 U.S. 457, 458.
2. *Trinity v. United States,* 143 U.S. 458–60.
3. *Trinity v. United States,* 143 U.S. 463–64.
4. *Trinity v. United States,* 143 U.S. 465.
5. *Trinity v. United States,* 143 U.S. AT 465–66.
6. *Trinity v. United States,* 143 U.S. AT 471.
7. *Trinity v. United States,* 143 U.S. AT 467–70.
8. *Trinity v. United States,* 143 U.S. AT 470–71.
9. *Trinity v. United States,* 143 U.S. AT 471.
10. *Trinity v. United States,* 143 U.S. AT 469–70.
11. *Trinity v. United States,* 143 U.S. AT 471.
12. *Trinity v. United States,* 143 U.S. AT 472.

Church of The Holy Trinity

vs.

United States

Church of The Holy Trinity
vs.
United States

No. 143.

SUPREME COURT OF THE UNITED STATES

143 U.S. 457, 36 L. Ed. 226, 12 S. Ct. 511

February 29, 1892, Decided

SYLLABUS

The act of February 26, 1885, "to prohibit the importation and migration of foreigners and aliens under contract or agreement to perform labor in the United States, its Territories, and the District of Columbia," 23 Stat. 322, c. 164, does not apply to a contract between an alien, residing out of the United States, and a religious society incorporated under the laws of a State, whereby he engages to remove to the United States and to enter into the service of the society as its rector or minister.

PRIOR HISTORY

ERROR TO THE CIRCUIT COURT OF THE UNITED STATES FOR
THE SOUTHERN DISTRICT OF NEW YORK.

STATEMENT OF THE CASE

The case is stated in the opinion.

COUNSEL

Mr. Seaman Miller for plaintiff in error.

Mr. Assistant Attorney General Maury for defendant in error submitted on his brief.

AUTHOR:
BREWER

OPINION

Mr. Justice Brewer delivered the opinion of the court.

Plaintiff in error is a corporation, duly organized and incorporated as a religious society under the laws of the State of New York. E. Walpole Warren was, prior to September, 1887, an alien residing in England. In that month the plaintiff in error made a contract with him, by which he was to remove to the city of New York and enter into its service as rector and pastor; and in pursuance of such contract, Warren did so remove and enter upon such service. It is claimed by the United States that this contract on the part of the plaintiff in error was forbidden by the act of February 26, 1885, 23 Stat. 332, c. 164, and an action was commenced to recover the penalty prescribed by that act. The Circuit Court held that the contract was within the prohibition of the statute, and rendered judgment accordingly, (36 Fed. Rep. 303;) and the single question presented for our determination is whether it erred in that conclusion.

The first section describes the act forbidden, and is in these words:

"Be it enacted by the Senate and House of Representatives of the United States of America in Congress assembled, That from and after the passage of this act it shall be unlawful for any person, company, partnership, or corporation, in any manner whatsoever, to prepay the transportation, or in any way assist or encourage the importation or migration of any alien or aliens, any foreigner or foreigners, into the United States, its Territories, or the District of Columbia, under contract or agreement, parol or special, express or implied, made previous to the importation or migration of such alien or aliens, foreigner or foreigners, to perform labor or service of any kind in the United States, its Territories, or the District of Columbia."

It must be conceded that the act of the corporation is within the letter of this section, for the relation of rector to his church is one of service, and implies labor on the one side with compensation on the other.

Not only are the general words labor and service both used, but also, as it were to guard against any narrow interpretation and emphasize a breadth of meaning, to them is added "of any kind;" and, further, as noticed by the Circuit Judge in his opinion, the fifth section, which makes specific exceptions, among them professional actors, artists, lecturers, singers and domestic servants, strengthens the idea that every other kind of labor and service was intended to be reached by the first section. While there is great force to this reasoning, we cannot think Congress intended to denounce with penalties a transaction like that in the present case. It is a familiar rule, that a thing may be within the letter of the statute and yet not within the statute, because not within its spirit, nor within the intention of its makers. This has been often asserted, and the reports are full of cases illustrating its application. This is not the substitution of the will of the judge for that of the legislator, for frequently words of general meaning are used in a statue, words broad enough to include an act in question, and yet a consideration of the whole legislation, or of the circumstances surrounding its enactment, or of the absurd results which follow from giving such broad meaning to the words, makes it unreasonable to believe that the legislator intended to include the particular act. As said in Plowden, 205: "From which cases, it appears that the sages of the law heretofore have construed statutes quite contrary to the letter in some appearance, and those statutes which comprehend all things in the letter they have expounded to extend to but some things, and those which generally prohibit all people from doing such an act they have interpreted to permit some people to do it, and those which include every person in the letter, they have adjudged to reach to some persons only, which expositions have always been founded upon the intent of the legislature; which they have collected sometimes by considering the cause and necessity of making the act, sometimes by comparing one part of the act with another, and sometimes by foreign circumstances."

In *Margate Pier Co. v. Hannam*, 3 B. & Ald. 266, 270, Abbott, C.J. quotes from Lord Coke as follows: "Acts of Parliament are to be so construed as no man that is innocent or free from injury or wrong be, by a literal construction, punished or endamaged." In the case of the *State v. Clark*, 5 Dutcher, (29 N.J. Law) 96, 98, 99, it appeared that an act had been passed making it a misdemeanor to wilfully break down a fence in the possession of another person. Clark was indicted under that statute. The defense was that the act of breaking down the fence, though wilful, was in the exercise of a legal right to go upon his own lands. The trial court rejected the testimony offered to sustain the defence, and the Supreme Court held that this ruling was error. In its opinion the court used this language: "The act of 1885, in terms, makes the wilful opening, breaking down or injuring of any fences belonging to or in the possession of any other person a misdemeanor. In what sense is the term wilful used? In common parlance, wilful is used in the sense of intentional, as distinguished from accidental or involuntary. Whatever one does intentionally he does wilfully. Is it used in that sense in this act? Did the legislature intend to make the intentional opening of a fence for the purpose of going upon the land of another indictable, if done by permission or for a lawful purpose?... We cannot suppose such to have been the actual intent. To adopt such a construction would put a stop to the ordinary business of life. The language of the act, if construed literally, evidently leads to an absurd result. If a literal construction of the words of a statute be absurd, the act must be so construed as to avoid the absurdity. The court must restrain the words. The object designed to be reached by the act must limit and control the literal import of the terms and phrases employed." In *United States v. Kirby*, 7 Wall. 482, 486, the defendants were indicted for the violation of an act of Congress, providing "that if any person shall knowingly and wilfully obstruct or retard the passage of the mail, or of any driver or carrier, or of any horse or carriage carrying the same, he shall, upon conviction, for every such offence pay a fine not exceeding one hundred dollars." The specific charge was that the defendants knowingly and wilfully retarded the passage of one Farris, a carrier of the mail, while engaged in the performance of his duty, and also in like manner retarded the steamboat General Buell, at that time engaged in carrying the mail. To this indictment the defendants pleaded specially that Farris had been indicted for murder by a court of competent authority in Kentucky; that a bench warrant had been issued and placed in the hands of the defendant Kirby, the sheriff of the county, commanding him to arrest Farris and bring him before the court to answer to the indictment; and that in obedience to this warrant, he and the other defendants, as his posse, entered upon the steamboat General Buell and arrested Farris, and used only such force as was necessary to accomplish that arrest. The question as to the sufficiency of this plea was certified to this court, and it was held that the arrest of Farris upon the warrant from the state court was not an obstruction of the mail, or the retarding of the passage of a carrier of the mail, within the meaning of the act. In its opinion the court says: "All laws should receive a sensible construction. General terms should be so limited in their application as not to lead to injustice, oppression or an absurd consequence. It will always, therefore, be presumed that the legislature intended exceptions to its language which would avoid results of this character. The reason of the law in such cases should prevail over its letter. The common sense of man approves the judgment mentioned by Puffendorf, that the Bolognian law which enacted 'that whoever drew blood in the streets should be punished with the utmost severity,' did not extend to the surgeon who opened the vein of a person that fell down in the street in a fit. The same common sense accepts the ruling, cited by Plowden, that the statute of 1st Edward II, which enacts that a prisoner who breaks prison shall be guilty of felony, does not extend to a prisoner who breaks out when the prison is on fire, 'for he is not to be hanged because he would not stay to be burnt.' And we think that a like common sense will sanction the ruling we make, that the act of Congress which punishes the obstruction or retarding of the passage of the mail, or of its carrier, does not apply to a case of temporary detention of the mail caused by the arrest of the carrier upon an indictment for murder." The following cases may also be cited. *Henry v. Tilson,* 17 Vermont, 479; *Ryegate v. Wardsboro,* 30 Vermont, 746; *Ex parte Ellis,* 11 California, 222; *Ingraham v. Speed,* 30 Mississippi, 410; *Jackson V. Collins,* 3 Cowen, 89; *People v. Insurance Company,* 15 Johns. 358; *Burch v. Newbury,* 10 N.Y. 374; *People v. N.Y. Commissioners of Taxes,* 95 N.Y. 554, 558; *People v. Lacombe,* 99 N.Y. 43, 49; *Canal Co. v. Railroad Co.,* 4 G. & J., 1, 152; *Osgood v. Breed,* 12 Mass. 525, 530; *Wilbur v. Crane,* 13 Pick. 284; *Oates v. National Bank,* 100 U.S. 239.

Among other things which may be considered in determining the intent of the legislature is the title of the act. We do not mean that it may be used to add to or take from the body of the statute, *Hadden v. The Collector,* 5 Wall. 107, but it may help to interpret its meaning. In the case of *United States v. Fisher,* 2 Cranch, 358, 386, Chief Justice Marshall said: "On the influence which the title ought to have in construing the enacting clauses much has been said; and yet it is not easy to discern the point of difference between the opposing counsel in this respect. Neither party contends that the title of an act can control plain words in the body of the statute; and neither denies that, taken with other parts, it may assist in removing ambiguities. Where the intent is plain, nothing is left to construction. Where the mind labors to discover the design of the legislature, it seizes everything from which aid can be derived; and in such case the title claims of degree of notice, and will have its due share of consideration."

And in the case of *United States v. Palmer,* 3 Wheat, 610, 631, the same judge applied the doctrine in this way: "The words of the section are in terms of unlimited extent. The words 'any person or persons' are broad enough to comprehend every human being. But general words must not only be limited to cases within the jurisdiction of the State, but also to those objects to which the legislature intended to apply them. Did the legislature intend to apply these words to the subjects of a foreign power, who in a foreign ship may commit murder or robbery on the high seas? The title of an act cannot control its words, but may furnish some aid in showing what was in the mind of the legislature. The title of this act is, 'An act for the punishment of certain crimes against the United States.' It would seem that offences against the United States, not offences against the human race, were the crimes which the legislature intended by this law to punish."

It will be seen that words as general as those used in the first section of this act were by that decision limited, and the intent of Congress with respect to the act was gathered partially, at least, from its title. Now, the title of this act is, "An act to prohibit the importation and migration of foreigners and aliens under contract or agreement to perform labor in the United States, its Territories and the District of Columbia." Obviously the thought expressed in this reaches only to the work of the manual laborer, as distinguished from that of the professional man. No one reading such a title would suppose that Congress had in its mind any purpose of staying the coming into this country of ministers of the gospel, or, indeed, of any class whose toil is that of the brain. The common understanding of the terms labor and laborers does not include preaching and preachers; and it is to be assumed that words and phrases are used in their ordinary meaning. So whatever of light is thrown upon the statute by the language of the title indicates any exclusion from its penal provisions of all contracts for the employment of ministers, rectors and pastors.

Again, another guide to the meaning of a statute is found in the evil which it is designed to remedy; and for this the court properly looks at contemporaneous events, the situation as it existed, and as it was pressed upon the attention of the legislative body. *United States v. Union Pacific Railroad,* 91 U.S. 72, 79. The situation which called for this statute was briefly but fully stated by Mr. Justice Brown when, as District Judge, he decided the case of *United States v. Craig,* 28 Fed. Rep. 795, 798: "The motives and history of the act are matters of common knowledge. It had become the practice for large capitalists in this country to contract with their agents abroad for the shipment of great numbers of an ignorant and servile class of foreign laborers, under contracts, by which the employer agreed, upon the one hand, to prepay their passage, while, upon the other hand, the laborers agreed to work after their arrival for a certain time at a low rate of wages. The effect of this was to break down the labor market, and to reduce other laborers engaged in like occupations to the level of the assisted immigrant. The evil finally became so flagrant that an appeal was made to Congress for relief by the passage of the act in question, the design of which was to raise the standard of foreign immigrants, and to discountenance the migration of those who had not sufficient means in their own hands, or those of their friends, to pay their passage."

It appears, also, from the petitions, and in the testimony presented before the committees of Congress, that it was this cheap unskilled labor which was making the trouble, and the influx of which Congress sought to prevent. It was never suggested that we had in this country a surplus of brain toilers, and, least of all, that the market for services of

Christian ministers was depressed by foreign competition. Those were matters to which the attention of Congress, or of the people, was not directed. So far, then, as the evil which was sought to be remedied interprets the statute, it also guides to an exclusion of this contract from the penalties of the act.

A singular circumstance, throwing light upon the intent of Congress, is found in this extract from the report of the Senate Committee on Education and Labor, recommending the passage of the bill: "The general facts and considerations which induce the committee to recommend the passage of this bill are set forth in the Report of the Committee of the House. The committee reports the bill back without ammendment, although there are certain features thereof which might well be changed or modified, in the hope that the bill may not fail of passage during the present session. Especially would the committee have otherwise recommended amendments, substituting for the expression 'labor and service,' whenever it occurs in the body of the bill, the words 'manual labor' or 'manual service,' as sufficiently broad to accomplish the purposes of the bill, and that such amendments would remove objections which a sharp and perhaps unfriendly criticism may urge to the proposed legislation. The committee, however, believing that the bill in its present form will be construed as including only those whose labor or service is manual in character, and being very desirous that the bill become a law before the adjournment, have reported the bill without change." 6059, Congressional Record, 48th Congress. And, referring back to the report of the Committee of the House, there appears this language: "It seeks to restrain and prohibit the immigration or importation of laborers who would have never seen our shores but for the inducements and allurements of men whose only object is to obtain labor at the lowest possible rate, regardless of the social and material well-being of our own citizens and regardless of the evil consequences which result to American laborers from such immigration. This class of immigrants care nothing about our institutions, and in many instances never even heard of them; they are men whose passage is paid by the importers; they come here under contract to labor for a certain number of years; they are ignorant of our social condition, and that they may remain so they are isolated and prevented from coming into contact with Americans. They are generally from the lowest social stratum, and live upon the coarsest food and in hovels of a character before unknown to American workmen. They, as a rule, do not become citizens, and are certainly not a desirable acquisition to the body politic. The inevitable tendency of their presence among us is to degrade American labor, and to reduce it to the level of the imported pauper labor." Page 5359, Congressional Record, 48th Congress.

We find, therefore, that the title of the act, the evil which was intended to be remedied, the circumstances surrounding the appeal to Congress, the reports of the committee of each house, all concur in affirming that the intent of Congress was simply to stay the influx of this cheap unskilled labor.

But beyond all these matters no purpose of action against religion can be imputed to any legislation, state or national, because this is a religious people. This is historically true. From the discovery of this continent to the present hour, there is a single voice making this affirmation. The commission to Christopher Columbus, prior to his sail westward, is from "Ferdinand and Isabella, by the grace of God, King and Queen of Castile," etc., and recites that "it is hoped that by God's assistance some of the continents and islands in the ocean will be discovered," etc. The first colonial grant, that [was] made to Sir Walter Raleigh in 1584, was from "Elizabeth, by the grace of God, of England, Fraunce and Ireland, queen, defender of the faith," etc; and the grand authorizing him to enact statutes for the government of the proposed colony provided that "they be not against the true Christian faith now professed in the Church of England." The first charter of Virginia, granted by King James I in 1606, after reciting the application of certain parties for a charter, commenced the grant in these words: "We, greatly commending, and graciously accepting of, their Desires for the Furtherance of so noble a Work, which may, by the Providence of Almighty God, hereafter tend to the Glory of his Divine Majesty, in propagating of Christian Religion to such People, as yet live in Darkness and miserable Ignorance of the true Knowledge and Worship of God, and may in time bring the Infidels and Savages, living in those parts, to human Civility, and to a settled and quiet Government; Do, by these our Letters-Patents, graciously accept of, and agree to, their humble and well-intended Desires."

Language of similar import may be found in the subsequent charters of that colony, from the same king, in 1609 and 1611; and the same is true of the various charters granted to the other colonies. In language more or less emphatic is the establishment of the Christian religion declared to be one of the purposes of the grant. The celebrated compact made by the Pilgrims in the Mayflower, 1620, recites: "Having undertaken for the Glory of God, and Advancement of the Christian Faith, and the Honour of our King and Country, a Voyage to plant the first Colony in the northern Parts of Virginia; Do by these Presents, solemnly and mutually, in the Presence of God and one another, covenant and combine ourselves together into a civil Body Politic, for our better Ordering and Preservation, and Furtherance of the Ends aforesaid."

The fundamental orders of Connecticut, under which a provisional government was instituted in 1638–1639, commence with this declaration: "Forasmuch as it hath pleased the Almighty God by the wise disposition of his divine providence so to Order and dispose of things that we the Inhabitants and Residents of Windsor, Hartford and Wethersfield are now cohabiting and dwelling in and upon the River of Conectecotte and the Lands thereunto adjoining; And well knowing where a people are gathered together the word of God requires that to maintain the peace and union of such a people there should be an orderly and decent Government established according to God, to order and dispose of the affairs of the people at all seasons as occasion shall require; do therefore associate and conjoin our souls to be as one Public State or Commonwealth; and do, for our souls and our Successors and such as shall be adjoined to us at any time hereafter, enter into Combination and Confederation together, to maintain and pressure the liberty and purity of the gospel of our Lord Jesus which we now profess, as also the discipline of the Churches, which according to the truth of the said gospel is now practised amongst us."

In the charter of privileges granted by William Penn to the province of Pennsylvania, in 1701, it is recited: "Because no People can be truly happy, though under the greatest Enjoyment of Civil Liberties, if abridged of the Freedom of their Consciences, as to their Religious Profession and

Worship; And Almighty God being the only Lord of Conscience, Father of Lights and Spirits; and the Author as well as Object of all divine Knowledge, Faith and Worship, who only doth enlighten the Minds, and persuade and convince the Understandings of People, I do hereby grant and declare," etc.

Coming nearer to the present time, the Declaration of Independence recognizes the presence of the Divine in human affairs in these words: "We hold these truths to be self-evident, that all men are created equal, that they are endowed by their Creator with certain unalienable Rights, that among these are Life, Liberty, and pursuit of Happiness.""We, therefore, the Representatives of the United States of America, in General Congress, Assembled, appealing to the Supreme Judge of the world for the rectitude of our intentions, do, in the Name and by Authority of the good People of these Colonies, solemnly publish and declare," etc.; "And for the support of this Declaration, with a firm reliance on the Protection of Divine Providence, we mutually pledge to each other our Lives, our Fortunes, and our sacred Honor."

If we examine the constitutions of the various States we find in them a constant recognition of religious obligations. Every constitution of every one of the forty-four States contains language which either directly or by clear implication recognizes a profound reverence for religion and an assumption that its influence in all human affairs is essential to the well being of the community. This recognition may be in the preamble, such as is found in the constitution of Illinois, 1870: "We, the people of the State of Illinois, grateful to Almighty God for the civil, political and religious liberty which He hath so long permitted us to enjoy, and looking to Him for a blessing upon our endeavors to secure and transmit the same unimpaired to succeeding generations," etc.

It may be only in the familiar requisition that all officers shall take an oath closing with the declaration "so help me God." It may be in clauses like that of the constitution of Indiana, 1816 Article XI, section 4: "The manner of administering an oath or affirmation shall be such as is most consistent with the conscience of the deponent, and shall be esteemed the most solemn appeal to God." Or in provisions such as are found in Articles 36 and 37 of the Declaration of Rights of the Constitution of

Maryland, 1867: "That as it is the duty of every man to worship God in such manner as he thinks most acceptable to Him, all persons are equally entitled to protection in their religious liberty; wherefore, no person ought, by any law, to be molested in his person or estate on account of his religious persuasion or profession, or for his religious practice, unless, under the color of religion, he shall disturb the good order, peace or safety of the State, or shall infringe the laws of morality, or injure others in their natural, civil or religious rights; nor ought any person to be compelled to frequent or maintain or contribute, unless on contract, to maintain any place of worship, or any ministry; nor shall any person, otherwise competent, be deemed incompetent as a witness, or juror, on account of his religious belief: Provided, He believes in the existence of God, and that, under His despensation, such person will be held morally accountable for his acts, and be rewarded or punished therefore, either in this world or the world to come. That no religious test ought ever to be required as a qualification for any office of profit or trust in this State other than a declaration of belief in the existence of God; nor shall the legislature prescribe any other oath of office than the oath prescribed by this constitution." Or like that in Articles 2 and 3, of Part 1st, of the Constitution of Massachusetts, 1780: "It is the right as well as the duty of all men in society publicly and at stated seasons, to worship the Supreme Being, the great Creator and Preserver of the universe....As the happiness of a people and the good order and preservation of civil government essentially depend upon piety, religion and morality, and as these cannot be generally diffused through a community but by the institution of the public worship of God and of public instructions in piety, religion and morality: Therefore, to promote their happiness and to secure the good order and preservation of their government, the people of this commonwealth have a right to invest their legislature with power to authorize and require, and the legislature shall, from time to time, authorize and require, the several towns, parishes, precincts and other bodies-politic or religious societies to make suitable provision, at their own expense, for the institution of the public worship of God and for the support and maintenance of public Protestant teachers of piety, religion and morality in all cases where such provision shall not be made voluntarily." Or as in sections 5 and 14 of Article 7, of the constitution of Mississippi, 1832: "No person who denies the being of a God, or a future state of rewards and punishments, shall hold any office in the civil department of this State.... Religion, morality and knowledge being necessary to good government, the preservation of liberty, and the happiness of mankind, schools and the means of education, shall forever be encouraged in this State." Or by Article 22 of the constitution of Delaware, 1776, which required all officers, besides an oath of allegiance, to make and subscribe the following declaration: "I, A.B., do profess faith in God the Father, and in Jesus Christ His only Son, and in the Holy Ghost, one God, blessed for evermore; and I do acknowledge the Holy Scriptures of the Old and New Testament to be given by divine inspiration."

Even the Constitution of the United States, which is supposed to have little touch upon the private life of the individual, contains in the First Amendment a declaration common to the constitutions of all the States, as follows: "Congress shall make no law respecting an establishment of religion, or prohibiting the free exercise thereof," etc. And also provides in Article 1, section 7, (a provision common to many constitutions,) that the Executive shall have ten days (Sundays excepted) within which to determine whether he will approve or veto a bill.

There is no dissonance in these declarations. There is a universal language pervading them all, having one meaning; they affirm and reaffirm that this a religious nation. These are not individual sayings, declarations of private persons: they are organic utterances; they speak the voice of the entire people. While because of a general recognition of this truth the question has seldom been presented to the courts, yet we find that in *Updegraph v. The Commonwealth*, 11 S. & R. 394, 400, it was decided that, "Christianity, general Christianity, is, and always had been, a part of the common law of Pennsylvania;...not Christianity with an established church, and tithes, and spiritual courts; but Christianity with liberty of conscience to all men." And in *The People v. Ruggles*, 8 Johns. 290, 294, 295, Chancellor Kent, the great commentator on American law, speaking as Chief Justice of the Supreme Court of New York, said: "The people of this State, in common with the people of this country, profess the general doctrines of Christianity, as the rule of their faith and practice;

and to scandalize the author of these doctrines is not only, in a religious point of view, extremely impious, but, even in respect to the obligations due to society, is a gross violation of decency and good order.... The free, equal and undisturbed enjoyment of religious opinion, whatever it may be, and free and decent discussions on any religious subject, is granted and recurred; but to revile, with malicious and blasphemous contempt, the religion professed by almost the whole community; is an abuse of that right. Nor are we bound, by any expressions in the Constitution as some have strangely supposed, either not to punish at all, or to punish indiscriminately, the like attacks upon the religion of Mahomet of the Grand Lama; and for this plain reason, that the case assumes that we are a Christian people, and the morality of the country is deeply engrafted upon Christianity, and not upon the doctrines or worship of those impostors." And in the famous case of Vidal v. Girard's Executors, 2 How. 127, 198, this court, while sustaining the will of Mr. Girard, with its provision for the creation of a college into which no minister should be permitted to enter, observed: "It is also said, and truly, that the Christian religion is a part of the common law of Pennsylvania."

If we pass beyond these matters to a view of American life as expressed by its laws, its business, its customs and its society, we find everywhere a clear recognition of the same truth. Among other matters note the following: The form of oath universally prevailing, concluding with an appeal to the Almighty; the custom of opening sessions of all deliberative bodies and most conventions with prayer; the prefatory words of all wills, "In the name of God, amen;" the laws respecting the observance of the Sabbath, with the general cessation of all secular business, and the closing of courts, legislatures, and other similar public assemblies on that day; the churches and church organizations which abound in every city, town and hamlet; the multitude of charitable organizations existing every where under Christian auspices; the gigantic missionary associations, with general support, and aiming to establish Christian missions in every quarter of the globe. These, and many other matters which might be noticed, add a volume of unofficial declarations to the mass of organic utterances that this is a Christian nation. In the face of all these, shall it be believed that a Congress of the United States intended to make it a misdemeanor for a church of this country to contract for the services of a Christian minister residing in another nation?

Suppose in the Congress that passed this act some member had offered a bill which in terms declared that, if any Roman Catholic church in this country should contract with Cardinal Manning to come to this country and enter into its service as pastor and priest; or any Episcopal church should enter into a like contract with Canon Farrar; or any Baptist church should make similar arrangements with Rev. Mr. Spurgeon; or any Jewish synagogue with some eminent Rabbi, such contract should be adjudged unlawful and void, and the church making it be subject to prosecution and punishment, can it be believed that it would have received a minute of approving thought or a single vote? Yet it is contended that such was in effect the meaning of this statute. The construction invoked cannot be accepted as correct. It is a case where there was presented a definite evil, in view of which the legislature used general terms with the purpose of reaching all phases of that evil, and thereafter, unexpectedly, it is developed that the general language thus employed is broad enough to reach cases and acts which the whole history and life of the country affirm could not have been intentionally legislated against. It is the duty of the counts, under those circumstances, to say that, however broad the language of the statute may be, the act, although within the letter, is not within the intention of the legislature, and therefore cannot be within the statute.

The judgment will be reversed, and the case remanded for further proceedings in accordance with this opinion.